Student Answer Key

GRASSROOTS WITH READINGS
The Writer's Workbook

EIGHTH EDITION

Student Answer Key

GRASSROOTS WITH READINGS
The Writer's Workbook

EIGHTH EDITION

Susan Fawcett

HOUGHTON MIFFLIN COMPANY   BOSTON   NEW YORK

Senior Sponsoring Editor: Lisa Kimball
Senior Development Editor: Judith Fifer
Editorial Associate: Peter Mooney
Editorial Assistant: Sage Anderson
Manufacturing Coordinator: Chuck Dutton
Marketing Manager: Annamarie Rice

Printed in the U.S.A.

ISBN: 0-618-50858-9

123456789-VHO-09 08 07 06 05

Contents

UNIT 1   **WRITING FORCEFUL PARAGRAPHS**   **1**

Chapter 3   Developing Effective Paragraphs   1
Chapter 4   Improving Your Paragraphs   2
Chapter 5   Moving from Paragraph to Essay   4
Unit 1   Review   5
Unit 1   Writers' Workshop   5

UNIT 2   **WRITING COMPLETE SENTENCES**   **6**

Chapter 6   Subjects and Verbs   6
Chapter 7   Avoiding Sentence Fragments   10
Unit 2   Review   15
Unit 2   Writers' Workshop   16

UNIT 3   **USING VERBS EFFECTIVELY**   **17**

Chapter 8   Present Tense (Agreement)   17
Chapter 9   Past Tense   25
Chapter 10   The Past Participle in Action   28
Chapter 11   Progressive Tenses (TO BE + -ING Verb Form)   34
Chapter 12   Fixed-Form Helping Verbs and Verb Problems   36
Unit 3   Review   39
Unit 3   Writers' Workshop   41

UNIT 4   **JOINING IDEAS TOGETHER**   **42**

Chapter 13   Coordination   42
Chapter 14   Subordination   43
Chapter 15   Avoiding Run-ons and Comma Splices   45
Chapter 16   Semicolons and Conjunctive Adverbs   50
Chapter 17   Relative Pronouns   53
Chapter 18   -ING Modifiers   54
Unit 4   Review   56
Unit 4   Writers' Workshop   58

UNIT 5   **CHOOSING THE RIGHT NOUN, PRONOUN, ADJECTIVE, ADVERB, OR PREPOSITION**   **59**

Chapter 19   Nouns   59
Chapter 20   Pronouns   63
Chapter 21   Adjectives and Adverbs   69
Chapter 22   Prepositions   73
Unit 5   Review   75
Unit 5   Writers' Workshop   76

UNIT 6   **REVISING FOR CONSISTENCY AND PARALLELISM**   **77**

Chapter 23   Consistent Tense   77
Chapter 24   Consistent Person   80
Chapter 25   Parallelism   81
Unit 6   Review   83
Unit 6   Writers' Workshop   85

UNIT 7   **MASTERING MECHANICS**   **86**

Chapter 26   Capitalization   86
Chapter 27   Commas   89
Chapter 28   Apostrophes   93
Chapter 29   Direct and Indirect Quotations   95
Chapter 30   Putting Your Proofreading Skills to Work   97
Unit 7   Review   103
Unit 7   Writers' Workshop   104

UNIT 8   **IMPROVING YOUR SPELLING**   **105**

Chapter 31   Spelling   105
Chapter 32   Look-Alikes/Sound-Alikes   109
Unit 8   Review   113
Unit 8   Writers' Workshop   114

APPENDIX 2 **SOME GUIDELINES FOR STUDENTS OF ENGLISH AS A SECOND LANGUAGE**   **115**

Count and Noncount Nouns   115
Verb + Gerund/Preposition + Gerund   115
Verb + Infinitive   116
Verb + Either Gerund or Infinitive   116

Student Answer Key

GRASSROOTS WITH READINGS
The Writer's Workbook

EIGHTH EDITION

UNIT 1
Writing Forceful Paragraphs

Chapter 3 Developing Effective Paragraphs

Part A. Defining the Paragraph and the Topic Sentence

Practice 1, page 16

The following letters should be circled:

1. c
2. e
3. e

4. a
5. d

Part B. Narrowing the Topic and Writing the Topic Sentence

Practice 2, page 19

The following topic sentences should be checked or rewritten:

1. √
2. Saving money requires discipline but has unexpected rewards.
3. It is hard to change some of the attitudes about food that we learn as children.
4. Being able to set my own study schedule in college has improved my attitude toward studying.
5. √

Part F. Writing and Revising the Paragraph

Practice 10, page 26

1. U
2. 3
3. 5

Part G. Writing the Final Draft

Practice 13, page 29

The following words should be added as shown:

1. People used to guess the time _^ day by watching the sun move across the sky. *of*

2. Sunrise and sunset were easy _^ recognize. *to*

3. Recognizing noon _^ easy, too. *was*

4. However, telling time by the position of _^ sun was very difficult at other times. *the*

5. C

6. They found it easier to tell time by looking at the shadows than by looking _^ the sun. *at*

7. People stuck poles into the ground to _^ time by the length of the shadows. *tell*

8. Those _^ the first shadow clocks, or sundials. *were*

9. In 300 BC, _^ Chaldean astronomer invented a more accurate, bowl-shaped sundial. *a*

10. Today, most sundials _^ decorative, but they can still be used to tell time. *are*

Chapter 4 Improving Your Paragraphs

Part A. More Work on Support: Examples

Practice 1, page 33

The following letters should be circled:

1. b   4. b
2. d   5. c
3. d

Practice 2, page 34

The following sentences are possible answers:

1. In *Independence Day,* for instance, a huge spaceship hovers over major cities.
2. The wedding on *Who Wants to Marry a Multi-Millionaire?* made a mockery of marriage.
3. On Tuesday, he bought a combination lint remover–beard brush; and on Thursday, he couldn't resist getting an automatic sauce-stirring device.
4. She sometimes walks up the stairs to her office on the twelfth floor.
5. My five-year-old niece Rachel once told me that God wears a blue nightshirt.

Part B. More Work on Arranging Ideas: Coherence

Practice 4, page 36

1. 2, 3, 4, 1
2. 1, 3, 4, 2, 5
3. 1, 4, 3, 2

Practice 6, page 37

1. 2 (3), 1 (4), 4 (1), 3 (2)
2. 3 (3), 2 (4), 4 (2), 1 (5), 5 (1)
3. 3 (3), 1 (5), 2 (4), 5 (1), 4 (2)

Practice 8, page 40

1. 2 (2), 3 (1), 1 (3)
2. 3, 1, 2
3. 2, 3, 1, 4

Part C. More Work on Revising: Exact and Concise Language

Practice 10, page 42

The following sentences are possible answers:

1. A late-model Infiniti roared down Maple Street.
2. This apartment has peeling paint and leaky water pipes.
3. When Allison walks in the door, her cat meows and rubs up against her leg.
4. This issue of *National Geographic* has beautiful photographs of wolves.
5. His reassuring eyes and warm smile made me feel comfortable.
6. Selling toe rings and ear cuffs to enthusiastic teenagers lifts my spirits.
7. A freak electrical storm swept through Cleveland last week.
8. Crying children, people with broken bones, and busy nurses fill the emergency room.

Practice 11, page 43

The following sentences are possible answers:

1. For hundreds of years, this beautiful city has been a major tourist attraction.
2. People go to Venice to see its priceless art and palaces, famous bridges, and canals that serve as streets.
3. Now, however, Venice is being destroyed by floods, polluted air and water, and tourists.
4. Twelve million visitors invade Venice every year, and most of them are day-trippers.
5. The day-trippers, who often bring their own drinks and sandwiches, contribute very little to the city's economy.
6. However, they contribute enormously to the city's congestion, transportation, and sanitation nightmares.
7. Recently, the city tried to scare off day-trippers through a negative publicity campaign.
8. Posters showed tourists being devoured by Venice's famous pigeons.

9. An giant toilet plunger became the symbol of the most romantic city in the world.
10. Unfortunately, the bad publicity did not stop tourists from pouring into Venice, so the city officials are trying a new plan—asking visitors to make reservations.

Part D. Turning Assignments into Paragraphs

Practice 14, page 46

The following are possible topic sentences:

1. Computer education should be required in every public high school.
2. A late-model used car can have all the advantages of a new car and save people a lot of money.
3. There is too much bad news on television news programs.
4. I have become more interested in both local and national politics in the past five years.

Practice 16, page 46

The following are possible topic sentences:

1. All high school graduates should be able to continue their higher education free of charge.
2. Expecting one's spouse to be perfect is one of the most important reasons for the high divorce rate in the United States.
3. Parents should give children an allowance so that they can learn how to handle money.
4. It is usually better to speak out on important issues than to remain silent.

Chapter 5 Moving from Paragraph to Essay

Part A. Defining the Essay and the Thesis Statement

Practice 1, page 50

The following are possible supporting points:

Paragraph 2
Point 1: didn't appreciate discipline
Point 2: yelling made me laugh
Point 3: didn't want to hurt people

Paragraph 3
Point 1: before—reacted to challenges
Point 2: after—saw danger realistically

Paragraph 4
Point 1: I am more confident.
Point 2: pussycat, not lion
Point 3: nothing to prove

Unit 1 Review

Choosing a Topic Sentence, page 56

The following letters should be circled:

1. c
2. d

Selecting Ideas, page 56

The following ideas should be checked "Keep":

1. on her TV show, often has experts who help people with relationships or finances
2. through her book club, inspired millions to start reading and periodically introduces a vast audience to new and old authors
3. proves that women don't need to be thin to be beautiful, popular, famous, and greatly loved
6. is a well-known example of someone who overcame many obstacles, including childhood abuse and racial prejudice
9. Winfrey gives millions to causes such as helping South African children orphaned by AIDS
10. Her website and magazine encourage women to develop their spirituality and pursue personal goals

The following ideas should be checked "Drop":

4. was born in 1954 on a farm in Mississippi
5. at age six was sent to Milwaukee; kept cockroaches in a jar as substitute for farm animals
7. another example of someone who has overcome abuse and prejudice is actress Halle Berry
8. physical abuse by a former boyfriend caused Berry to lose 80 percent of her hearing in one ear

Examining a Paragraph, page 57

The following answers should be given:

1. 1
2. order of importance
3. (a) 3, 4, 6 (b) 4 and 6

Unit 1 Writers' Workshop, page 58

Discuss Your Name

1. N   Y
   Y   Y
4. No, she should drop the first sentence and begin with "My name YuMing . . ."
6. time order

UNIT 2
Writing Complete Sentences

Chapter 6 Subjects and Verbs

Part A. Defining and Spotting Subjects

Practice 1, page 63

The following subjects are possible choices:

1. hockey puck
2. student
3. spy
4. comic books

5. wallpaper
6. Papers, pencils
7. singer, voice
8. farmhouse, ceiling, downstairs windows

Practice 2, page 63

The following complete subjects should be circled:

1. Dr. Leon Rappoport
2. Humans
3. movies
4. psychologists
5. People

6. films and stories
7. moviegoers
8. teenagers
9. parents
10. adolescents

Practice 3, page 64

The following sentences are possible answers:

1. The gymnasts trained day and night for the big event.
2. Ricky Martin has a dynamic singing voice.
3. A small plane landed in the cornfield.
4. After the show, the crowd applauded and screamed for fifteen minutes.
5. Mr. Sandhurst got out of the large gray van.

Part B. Spotting Singular and Plural Subjects

Practice 4, page 65

The following columns should be checked:

1.	plural	5.	plural
2.	plural	6.	plural
3.	singular	7.	plural
4.	singular	8.	singular

Practice 5, page 65

The following complete subjects should be circled and labeled:

1.	Aaron McGruder	S
2.	Comic books and hip hop music	P
3.	existing comics	P
4.	McGruder	S
5.	The characters	P
6.	The strip	S
7.	Rave reviews and a few angry letters	P
8.	A major music magazine	S
9.	Expanding racial dialogue by using humor	S
10.	The daily strip, a book, and TV projects	P

Part C. Spotting Prepositional Phrases

Practice 6, page 67

The following prepositional phrases should be crossed out and the subjects circled:

1. That famous (trail) stretches ~~from Springer Mountain in Georgia to Mount Katahdin in Maine~~.

2. One-(quarter) ~~of the trail~~ goes ~~through Virginia~~.

3. The (majority) ~~of walkers~~ hike ~~for one day~~.

4. ~~Of the four million trail users~~, two hundred (people) complete the entire trail every year.

5. ~~For most hikers~~, the (trip) ~~through fourteen states~~ takes four or five months.

6. ~~In the spring~~, many hardy (souls) begin their 2,158-mile-long journey.

7. These (lovers) ~~of the wilderness~~ must reach Mount Katahdin ~~before winter~~.

8. ~~On the trail,~~ (men and women) battle heat, humidity, bugs, blisters, muscle sprains, and food and water shortages.

9. After beautiful green scenery, the (path) becomes rocky and mountainous.

10. (Hikers) in the White Mountains of New Hampshire struggle against high winds.

11. A (pebble) from Georgia is sometimes added to the pile of stones at the top of Mount Katahdin.

12. At the bottom of the mountain, the (conquerors) of the Appalachian Trail add their names to the list of successful hikers.

Part D. Defining and Spotting Action Verbs

Practice 7, page 68

The following action verbs are possible choices:

1. sailed
2. sketched
3. crowed, barked
4. raged, howled

5. clapped, bowed
6. chops, slices
7. broke, cheered
8. slides, glides

Practice 8, page 68

The following action verbs should be circled:

1. explodes
2. survived
3. brought
4. sat, wrote
5. finished

6. sell
7. tells
8. attracts, enthralls
9. began

Part E. Defining and Spotting Linking Verbs

Practice 9, page 69

The following linking verbs should be circled:

1. sounds
2. was
3. appeared

4. felt
5. became

Practice 10, page 70

The following linking verbs should be circled and the subjects and descriptive words underlined:

1. The sweet potato pie (tastes) delicious.

2. You usually (seem) energetic.

3. During the summer, she (looks) calm.

4. Under heavy snow, <u>the new dome roof</u> (appeared) sturdy.

5. <u>Raphael</u> (is) <u>a gifted animal trainer</u>.

6. Lately, <u>I</u> (feel) <u>very competent</u> at work.

7. <u>Luz</u> (became) <u>a medical technician</u>.

8. <u>Yvonne</u> (acted) <u>surprised</u> at her baby shower.

Part F. Spotting Verbs of More Than One Word

Practice 11, page 71

The following complete verbs should be listed and the main verbs circled:

1. has (worked)
2. can be (used)
3. is (believed)
4. can (select)
5. might (show)

6. will (shout)
7. has been (practicing)
8. are (learning)
9. can be (taught)
10. are (excited)

Practice 12, page 71

The following subjects should be boxed, the main verbs circled, and the helping verbs underlined:

1. [Scientists] <u>have</u> (developed) one theory.

2. According to this theory, the [universe] (began) with a huge explosion.

3. The [explosion] <u>has been</u> (named) the Big Bang.

4. First, all [matter] <u>must have been</u> (packed) into a tiny speck under enormous pressure.

5. Then, about 15 billion years ago, that [speck] (burst) with amazing force.

6. [Everything] in the universe <u>has</u> (come) from the original explosion.

7. In fact, the [universe] still <u>is</u> (expanding) from the Big Bang.

8. [All] of the planets and stars <u>are</u> (moving) away from each other at an even speed.

9. <u>Will</u> [it] (expand) forever?

10. [Experts] <u>may be</u> (debating) that question for a long time.

Chapter Review, page 72

The following subjects should be circled, prepositional phrases crossed out, and complete verbs underlined:

Target Practice

(1) Successful people know an important secret about setting and reaching goals. (2) These high achievers break their goals down into smaller, more manageable steps or targets. (3) Hitting these targets one by one will lead them to the goal. (4) On the other hand, huge goals overwhelm most people. (5) These might include graduating from college, becoming a bank president, or hitting forty home runs in one season.

(6) In order to break down a major goal into small steps, many achievers start by thinking backward. (7) Dillon's goal, for example, was to lose twenty pounds by graduation. (8) In order to lose that much weight, Dillon decided to set smaller targets for himself. (9) His first target was to reduce his eating between meals. (10) No snacks would be allowed except an apple or other low-calorie fruit to calm a major craving. (11) Dillon's second target was to avoid going back for second helpings at any meal—no matter what. (12) Taking a walk every evening after dinner became his third target. (13) At night, Dillon checked off the targets hit that day.

(14) Even high achievers do not complete a major goal, like losing a lot of weight, every day. (15) However, they feel satisfaction about moving forward, one small step at a time. (16) The photographer at Dillon's graduation captured his beaming smile. (17) Under that cap and gown, Dillon's weight had dropped by twenty-two pounds.

Chapter 7 Avoiding Sentence Fragments

Part A. Writing Sentences with Subjects and Verbs

Practice 1, page 75

The following answers are possible choices:

1. On a hot day in Alabama, butter melts easily.
2. That couple on the street corner just won the lottery.

3. One of the fans caught a fly ball.
4. My next-door neighbor manages a Software City store.
5. The tip of her nose was red from the cold.
6. DVD players are replacing VCRs in many homes.
7. Parking my car at the airport all week makes me nervous.
8. Edgardo is a person who likes to take risks.

Part B. Writing Sentences with Complete Verbs

Practice 2, page 76

The following sentences are possible answers:

1. The Australian is winning the tennis match.
2. Her parents have gone to the movies.
3. Steve's letter was published in the *Miami Herald.*
4. My physics professor is always forgetting the assignment.
5. This sari is made of scarlet silk.
6. For the past two years, Joan has been working at a computer company.
7. Have you ever been to Alaska?
8. Yesterday, Ed's wet gloves were taken from the radiator.

Practice 3, page 77

The following sentences are possible answers:

1. The spy has forgotten the password.
2. Students are now running the copy center.
3. Jim is making sculpture from old car parts.
4. My aunt has been working at the state capitol building.
5. Two cats are creeping along the windowsill.
6. Phil Hamilton has driven that tractor for years.
7. My sister and I slept through the TV program.
8. None of my friends had been to a wrestling match.

Practice 4, page 77

The following numbers should be circled and errors corrected:

(1) On a routine day in 1946, a scientist at the Raytheon Company *put* his hand into his pants pocket for a candy bar. (2) The chocolate, however, *was* a messy, sticky mass of gunk. (3) Dr. Percy Spencer had been testing a magnetron tube. (4) Could the chocolate have melted from radiation leaking from the tube? (5) Spencer sent out for a bag of popcorn kernels. (6) *He put* the kernels near the tube. (7) Within minutes, corn *was* popping wildly onto the lab floor. (8) Within a short time,

was

Raytheon working on the development of the microwave oven. ((9))Microwave cooking the first
                ^   became
                                                                                        ^
                                                                                    It was
new method of preparing food since the discovery of fire more than a million years ago. ((10)) Was

the first cooking technique that did not directly or indirectly apply fire to food.

Part C. Completing the Thought

Practice 5, page 79

The following choices are possible answers:

1. she bumped into her old boyfriend.
2. please take me with you.
3. Maurie did his math homework.
4. you will succeed.
5. I find them fascinating.
6. I do not want to have it.
7. I think of Billie Holiday.
8. we have to keep them on all night.

Practice 6, page 79

The following choices are possible answers:

1. make me laugh.
2. seem unreal.
3. will compete in the Olympics.
4. often very funny.
5. often can help others.
6. starts to bark five minutes before I get home.
7. offer e-mail and other Internet services.
8. was rented from Video Watch.
9. should never go into sales.
10. is Kenya.

Practice 7, page 79

The following sentences are possible answers:

1. Are they visiting the White House?
2. That digital clock has been blinking for hours.
3. People who never say no to their children will probably regret not doing so.
4. Tanya and Jerry make tables from driftwood they find on the beach.
5. The squirrel scampered over the roof and into the garden.
6. Raúl completed a culinary arts program, and now he is a well-known chef.
7. Six-year-old Eric loves chess, which is a difficult game to play.
8. Whenever Dolly starts to yodel, her dog starts to howl.

Practice 8, page 80

The following numbers should be circled and errors corrected:

(1) The Special Olympics is an international ~~program.~~ *program* (2) ~~That~~ *that* is held for mentally

disabled children and adults. (3) Special Olympics athletes train and compete in regular ~~sports.~~ *sports,* (4) ~~Which~~ *which* include floor hockey, skiing, soccer, swimming, speed skating, and tennis.

(5) The Special Olympics winter and summer international games are held every other year. (6) Although 150 countries participate in the world ~~games.~~ *games, Special* (7) ~~Special~~ Olympics are also held

yearly at local and state levels. (8) Altogether, more than a million athletes participate.

(9) Whereas Special Olympics competitors may not swim as fast or jump as high as Olympic ~~stars.~~ *stars,* (10) ~~They~~ *they* are very eager to do their best. (11) Their courage and accomplishments inspire ~~everyone.~~ *everyone* (12) ~~And~~ *and* change these athletes' lives forever.

Chapter Review, page 81

The following numbers should be circled and errors corrected:

A. (1) Steel drums *are* wonderful and unusual musical instruments. (2) Steel bands use them to perform calypso, jazz, ~~and~~ popular ~~music.~~ *music,* (3) ~~And~~ *and* even classical symphonies. (4) Steel drums were invented in ~~Trinidad.~~ *Trinidad,* (5) ~~Where~~ *where* they were made from the ends of discarded oil ~~drums.~~ *drums* (6) ~~That~~ *that* had been left by the British navy. (7) Although the first steel drums produced only ~~rhythm.~~ *rhythm, now* (8) ~~Now~~ they can be tuned to play up to five octaves. (9) Steel orchestras produce ~~music.~~ *music* (10) ~~That~~ *that* surrounds and delights listeners without the use of amplifiers. (11) The worldwide popularity of steel drums has been increasing steadily. (12) The Trinidad All Steel Percussion Orchestra was a smash ~~hit.~~ *hit* (13) ~~When~~ *when* it first performed in England a number of years ago. (14) Recently, the Northern Illinois University Steel Band has been thrilling audiences from the United States to Taiwan.

B. (1) Many people seem to forget all about good ~~manners.~~ *manners* (2) ~~When~~ *when* they use a cell phone.

(3) They rudely allow the ringing phone to interrupt conversations, meetings, appointments,

performances, and romantic dinner dates. (4) Some even answer calls in church or at ~~funerals~~. *funerals and*

(5) ~~And~~ then proceed to talk ~~loudly~~. (6) ~~Forcing~~ others to listen or wait for them to finish talking. *loudly,* *forcing*

(7) Public relations consultant Carol ~~Page~~, known as the "Miss Manners of Cell Phones." (8) She *Page is*

created ~~cellmanners.com~~. (9) ~~Which~~ is a website promoting cell phone courtesy and civility. *cellmanners.com,* *which*

(10) Page believes that in order to stop cell ~~rudeness~~. (11) ~~We~~ should fix a "cell glare" on any cell *rudeness, we*

user who is behaving badly. (12) If that doesn't ~~work~~. (13) ~~We~~ can interrupt and gently ask if the *work, we*

phone conversation might be postponed. (14) Setting a good example when you use your own cell

phone ∧ probably the best way to teach good cellular phone manners to others. *is*

C. (1) Braille, which is a system of reading and writing now used by blind people all over the

~~world~~. (2) ~~Was~~ invented by a fifteen-year-old French boy. (3) In 1824, when Louis Braille entered *world, was*

a school for the blind in ~~Paris~~. (4) ~~He~~ found that the library had only fourteen books for the blind. *Paris, he*

(5) These books used a system that he and the other blind students found hard to use. (6) Most of

them just gave up. (7) Louis Braille devoted himself to finding a better way. (8) Working with the

French army method called ~~night-writing~~. (9) ~~He~~ came up with a new system in 1829. *night-writing, he*

(10) Although his classmates liked and used ~~Braille~~. (11) ~~It~~ not widely accepted in England and *Braille,* *it was*

the United States for another hundred years.

D. (1) Not all employers have a problem with employees who sleep on the job. (2) In fact,

when workers get that after-lunch draggy ~~feeling~~. (3) ~~Some~~ employers encourage them to nap. *feeling, some*

(4) Sleep researchers believe that people have a natural tendency to fall ~~asleep~~. (5) ~~During~~ the *asleep* *during*

afternoon. (6) Short naps energize ~~workers~~. (7) ~~And~~ improve both safety and performance. (8) Of *workers* *and*

course, nappers always have found ways to catch a few winks. (9) They snooze at (or under) desks

and in cars, closets, cafeterias, meeting rooms, and bathroom stalls. (10) Now, however, more and

more companies ∧ providing "relaxation rooms" and "nap nooks." (11) Camille and Bill Anthony, *are*

authors of *The Art of Napping at Work*, are even promoting a new holiday, National Workplace

Napping Day. (12) Because it falls on the Monday after the end of daylight-saving ~~time~~. *time,*

(13) ~~Employees~~ can make up the lost hour of sleep by napping at work. (14) To learn more, read the *employees*

book,   *which*
Anthonys' ~~book.~~ ((15)) ~~Which~~ includes chapters on napping places, napping policies, and the future

of workplace napping!

Unit 2 Review

Proofreading and Revising, page 84

The following corrections should be made:

Living Without Television

(1) What would you do without your television? (2) Every spring, millions of Americans

themselves   *by*
answer this question for ~~themselves.~~ ((3)) ~~By~~ taking part in the TV-Turnoff Week. (4) They find out

that they can in fact lead enjoyable lives without watching TV. (5) Begun in 1995, TV-Turnoff

days   *engaging*
Week now has motivated 24 million participants to spend seven full ~~days.~~ ((6)) ~~Engaging~~ in

activities other than TV viewing. ((7)) Although many TV-Turnoff Week participants fear that

TVs, they
they will be bored without their ~~TVs.~~ (8) ~~They~~ often rediscover the joys of reading, talking to

family and friends, going for walks, exercising, and learning new skills like playing the guitar.

(9) Statistics help explain the power of TV-Turnoff Week. (10) Americans watch more than

four hours of TV a day. (11) That's two full months each year. (12) Simply turning off the box

leaves people with lots of time to do other things. (13) Nearly half of the population watches TV

dinner   *instead*
while eating ~~dinner.~~ ((14)) ~~Instead~~ of using that time to talk to other family members. ((15)) ~~Because~~

bedrooms, they
56 percent of children have a television set in their ~~bedrooms.~~ (16) ~~They~~ tend to watch programs

alone instead of doing homework, interacting with their parents and siblings, or exercising.

(17) Interestingly, the consequences of TV-Turnoff Week seem to be lasting. (18) Many past

participants say that they have changed their viewing habits. ((19)) While a few people go so far

televisions, most   *shows*   *and*
as to get rid of their ~~televisions.~~ (20) ~~Most~~ report that they now watch fewer ~~shows.~~ ((21)) ~~And~~ are

less likely to leave their TV sputtering as unwatched background noise. (22) Some move their

televisions,   *taking*
~~televisions.~~ ((23)) ~~Taking~~ them out of bedrooms and the family room. (24) Others cancel or reduce

their cable or satellite services. (25) One major benefit is that individuals and families prove to themselves that they find other, more engaging things to do. (26) Many parents gain confidence about limiting their children's viewing *time* time. (27) *and,* And more important, about teaching their children how and when to watch TV.

Unit 2 Writers' Workshop, page 86

1. Y Y
    Y Y
4. time order
7. Yes, sentence fragments.

UNIT 3
Using Verbs Effectively

Chapter 8 Present Tense (Agreement)

Part A. Defining Agreement

Practice 1, page 91

The following present tense verbs should be listed:

1. asks
2. decides
3. remembers
4. wears

5. hopes
6. laughs
7. studies
8. amazes

Practice 2, page 91

The following verb forms should be listed:

to find	to ask	to go
finds	ask	goes
find	asks	go
find	asks	go

to rest	to hold	to select
rest	holds	selects
rest	hold	selects
rests	hold	select

Practice 3, page 91

The following subjects should be underlined and the verb forms circled:

1. <u>we</u> (fail)

2. <u>they</u> (differ)

3. <u>she</u> (describes)

4. <u>She</u> (reads) (finds)

5. She meets

6. she praises

7. she goes

8. he submits

9. She thinks

10. He believes

11. they represent

12. she criticizes

13. he expects

14. they cause

15. You decide

Part B. Troublesome Verb in the Present Tense: TO BE

Practice 4, page 93

The following forms of *to be* should be listed:

1. is
2. are, is
3. are, are
4. are
5. is
6. am
7. is, is
8. am, are
9. are
10. is, is
11. are
12. is
13. are
14. am, is
15. is, are

Part C. Troublesome Verb in the Present Tense: TO HAVE

Practice 5, page 94

The following present tense forms of *to have* should be listed:

1. has
2. have
3. have
4. has, have
5. has, has
6. have, have
7. have, have
8. have, has
9. has, have
10. have, have

Part D. Troublesome Verb in the Present Tense: TO DO (+ NOT)

Practice 6, page 95

The following present tense forms of *to do* should be listed:

1. does
2. do
3. does
4. do
5. do
6. do, do
7. does
8. do
9. Do
10. Does

Practice 7, page 95

The following positive and negative forms of *TO DO* should be listed:

1. does, doesn't
2. do, don't
3. do, don't
4. do, don't

5. does, doesn't
6. do, don't
7. does, doesn't
8. do, don't

Practice 8, page 95

The following present tense forms of *TO DO + NOT* should be listed:

1. don't
2. doesn't
3. don't
4. doesn't
5. don't

6. doesn't, don't
7. doesn't, don't
8. don't
9. don't, doesn't
10. don't, don't

Practice 9, page 96

The following present tense forms of *BE, HAVE,* or *DO* should be listed:

1. has, is
2. is, is
3. has
4. does, is
5. has, does, is

6. does
7. does
8. does
9. is
10. are

Part E. Changing Subjects to Pronouns

Practice 10, page 97

The following pronouns should be listed:

1. it
2. they
3. she
4. we
5. you

6. it
7. they
8. he
9. it
10. it

Practice 11, page 97

The following pronouns should be listed and the present tense verbs circled:

1. she (owns)
2. it (is)
3. you (seem)
4. we (repair)
5. it (grates)

6. it (is)
7. it (jams)
8. it (is)
9. they (are)
10. we (like)

Part F. Practice in Agreement

Practice 12, page 98

The following verbs should be circled:

1.	Do, is	11.	figure
2.	is	12.	think, are
3.	allow	13.	influence
4.	say, build	14.	publishes
5.	sell	15.	introduce
6.	exist	16.	are
7.	see	17.	have
8.	use	18.	want
9.	offers, make	19.	publishes, encourages
10.	has	20.	helps

Practice 13, page 100

The following verb forms are possible answers:

1.	attend	4.	leaps, spins
2.	encourages	5.	yip, woof
3.	compete	6.	goes

Practice 14, page 100

The following sentences should be listed:

1. The movie tickets cost too much.
2. The pipelines carry oil from Alaska.
3. White horses graze by the fence.
4. My brothers know American Sign Language.
5. The families need good health insurance.
6. The backup singers wear green contact lenses.
7. My nieces want an iguana.
8. Waves lap softly against the dock.

Practice 15, page 101

The following sentences should be listed:

1. My cousin raises sheep.
2. The engine roars loudly.
3. The student manages money wisely.
4. The inmate watches *America's Most Wanted.*
5. Overhead, a seagull rides on the wind.
6. A good card player knows when to bluff.
7. On Saturday, the pharmacist stays late.
8. The jewel from Bangkok is on display.

Practice 16, page 101

The following verbs should be corrected:

                                 watches   *whacks*

(1) A six-month-old in a highchair <u>watched</u> intently as his father <u>whacked</u> golf balls into a

                     starts   *give*

net in the family garage. (2) When the baby <u>started</u> to walk, his parents <u>gave</u> him a short putter,

      drags   *is*   *picks*

which he <u>dragged</u> around the house. (3) When he <u>was</u> nine months old, he carefully <u>picked</u> up the

              does   *swings*   *sends*

putter. (4) The child <u>did</u> an exact imitation of his father's hip swivel, <u>swung</u>, and <u>sent</u> the ball

                                     realize   *have*

perfectly into the net. (5) Thunderstruck, the father and mother <u>realized</u> that they <u>had</u> a golf

                                           practices

genius on their hands. (6) From the age of eighteen months, the toddler <u>practiced</u> his pitch and

                                   exclaims   *wants*

putt strokes on a golf course. (7) At age three, on a TV show, the boy <u>exclaimed</u> that he <u>wanted</u> to

                     does

beat Jack Nicklaus some day. (8) In fact, he <u>did</u> that at age twenty-one, winning the Masters with

                                         know

the lowest score in tournament history. (9) Suddenly, people all over the world <u>knew</u> the name

                         shatters

Tiger Woods. (10) At twenty-four, Tiger <u>shattered</u> U.S. Open records by a twelve under par and a

     ties

fifteen-stroke victory and <u>tied</u> Nicklaus's record of the lowest score ever in a U.S. Open. (11) His

     is   *see*   *has*

influence <u>was</u> enormous. (12) Young people <u>saw</u> golf as exciting, and the game <u>had</u> thousands of

new fans.

Part G. Special Problems in Agreement

Practice 17, page 103

The following prepositional phrases should be crossed out and the verbs circled:

1. ~~in my yard~~ (squawk)
2. ~~along Clark Street~~ (blink)
3. ~~of the repairs~~ (seems)
4. ~~with teenagers~~ (amazes)
5. ~~on his résumé~~ (show)

6. ~~to success~~ (is)
7. ~~of many illnesses~~ (is)
8. ~~in the zoo~~ (misses)
9. ~~from Kenya~~ (run)
10. ~~on the fifth floor~~ (have)

Practice 18, page 104

The following verbs should be circled:

1. is
2. wears
3. carries
4. sounds
5. sees

6. costs
7. is
8. commits
9. does
10. has

Practice 20, page 105

The following verbs should be circled:

1. is
2. is
3. are
4. is
5. are

6. is
7. are
8. are
9. are
10. is

Practice 21, page 106

The following sentences should be listed:

1. A daycare center is on campus.
2. A scarecrow hangs near the barn.
3. Two scarecrows are near the barn.
4. One good reason to quit this job is my supervisor.
5. Six customers are waiting ahead of you.
6. A water fountain is in the lounge.
7. A house and a barn stand in the wheat field.
8. Only two shopping days are left before my birthday.
9. Thousands of plant species grow in the rain forest.
10. A single blue egg is in the nest over the kitchen door.

Practice 22, page 106

The following verbs should be circled:

1. is
2. Has
3. are
4. are
5. is

6. does
7. Have
8. are
9. Has
10. do

Practice 24, page 107

The following verbs should be circled and subjects listed:

1.	fetches	robot
2.	have	cans
3.	takes	husband
4.	are	women
5.	sits	house
6.	love	students
7.	thinks	person
8.	flies	airline
9.	live	people
10.	challenge	jobs

Practice 25, page 108

The following present tense verbs should be underlined and/or corrected:

admire
(1) Many people who <u>love</u> exciting theater <u>admires</u> Anna Deveare Smith. (2) She <u>is</u> well

explore
known for her thought-provoking plays. (3) Many of these dramas <u>explores</u> social conflicts in

America, bringing important issues to live through the voices of different characters. (4) Smith's

probes
newest play, *House Arrest: First Edition,* <u>probe</u> the relationship between the media and the

White House. (5) Politicians, journalists, and worried citizens, played by a variety of actors, all

<u>speak</u> out. (6) In other shows, Smith brilliantly <u>plays</u> all the roles herself. (7) For example, one

examines
show, *Twilight: Los Angeles 1992,* <u>examine</u> the L.A. riots and the beatings of Rodney King and

Reginald Denny. (8) Smith, who <u>is</u> African American, movingly <u>expresses</u> the feelings of white

people, black people, Korean shopkeepers, angry rioters, and frightened citizens. (9) Once a shy

and withdrawn child, Anna Deveare Smith <u>works</u> to open herself to the experiences of others.

believes   *require*
(10) She <u>believe</u> that both successful acting and successful democracy <u>requires</u> us to grow in

tolerance.

Chapter Review, page 109

The following present tense verbs should be underlined and/or corrected:

Advantages and Disadvantages of Online Dating

(1) Every month, about 40 million Americans <u>visits</u> *visit* online dating sites like Match.com and Matchmaker.com. (2) In fact, these sites now <u>make</u> more money than any other paid service on the Web. (3) Clearly, many people no longer <u>feels</u> *feel* embarrassed about using a dating service. (4) But <u>are</u> websites really good places to find a mate? (5) You <u>decide</u>. (6) There <u>is</u> *are* both advantages and disadvantages to cyberdating.

(7) Some busy people <u>likes</u> *like* the convenience of online dating and the chance to meet people at any time of day or night. (8) The Web <u>makes</u> a better meeting place than bars, they <u>argue</u>. (9) In addition, the sites <u>allow</u> individuals to search for mates with certain qualities or characteristics. (10) According to supporters of cyberdating, this method also <u>encourage</u> *encourages* people to get to know possible romantic partners better. (11) In cyberspace, they <u>are</u> less likely to be swept away by physical attraction alone.

(12) However, computer dating also <u>have</u> *has* dangers and drawbacks. (13) Online, many people <u>tends</u> *tend* to lie about their physical appearance, age, profession, or personality traits. (14) According to a recent study, about three out of ten people using online sites <u>are</u> married. (15) Others <u>has</u> *have* criminal backgrounds. (16) Therefore, safety <u>remain</u> *remains* a constant concern for cyberdaters. (17) Getting to know each other online <u>takes</u> more time. (18) Consequently, the online environment actually <u>slow</u> *slows* down the dating process instead of speeding it up.

Chapter 9 Past Tense

Part A. Regular Verbs in the Past Tense

Practice 1, page 111

The following verbs should be circled and tenses listed:

1.	stroked	past
2.	travels	present
3.	donate	present
4.	sailed	past
5.	looks	present
6.	buried	past
7.	erupted	past
8.	pollutes	present
9.	nested	past
10.	owns	present

Practice 2, page 112

The following verbs should be changed to past tense:

transformed
(1) Again this year, Carnival *transforms* Rio de Janeiro, Brazil, into one of the most fantastic

four-day parties on the planet. (2) On the Friday before Ash Wednesday, thousands of visitors
poured   watched   admired
pour into the city. (3) They *watch* all-night parades and *admire* the glittering costumes. (4) They
cheered sweated   danced   started
cheer, *sweat*, and *dance* the samba. (5) Of course, preparation *starts* long before. (6) For months,
                                        planned   practiced
members of the samba schools (neighborhood dance clubs) *plan* their floats, *practice* samba steps,
     stayed
and *stay* up for nights making their costumes. (7) Using bright fabrics, sequins, feathers, and
                              created   constructed
chains, both men and women *create* spectacular outfits. (8) Each samba school *constructs* a float
     featured   rated
that *features* a smoke-breathing dragon or spouting waterfall. (9) During Carnival, judges *rate* the
                                        awarded
schools on costumes, dancing, and floats, and then *award* prizes. (10) Together, Brazilians and
          shared
their visitors *share* great music, drink, food, fun, and the chance to go a little bit crazy.

Practice 3, page 112

The following past tense verb forms are possible choices:

1.	helped		4.	pounded, installed
2.	arrived		5.	worked, learned
3.	grabbed, climbed		6.	cried, thanked

Practice 4, page 113

The following past tense verb forms should be listed:

1. dreamed
2. laughed
3. gathered, started
4. reached, slipped, survived
5. stumbled, wondered
6. vowed
7. battled
8. managed, edged
9. stepped, stayed
10. symbolized

Part B. Irregular Verbs in the Past Tense

Practice 5, page 115

The following past tense verb forms should be listed:

1. grew
2. went
3. lay
4. sought
5. taught
6. was
7. flew
8. made
9. kept
10. set
11. wrote
12. became

Practice 6, page 115

The following past tense verb forms should be listed:

1. began
2. thought
3. spent, read
4. did
5. spoke, had
6. understood, wrote
7. told
8. gave
9. chose
10. were, knew
11. felt, got
12. put
13. took
14. rang, made

Part C. Troublesome Verb in the Past Tense: TO BE

Practice 8, page 117

The following past tense forms of the verb *to be* should be circled:

1. was
2. were
3. was
4. were
5. was, was
6. was, were
7. were, was
8. Were
9. were, was
10. were

Practice 9, page 117

The following past tense forms of the verb *TO BE + NOT* should be listed:

1. weren't
2. wasn't
3. wasn't
4. wasn't
5. weren't
6. wasn't
7. wasn't
8. wasn't
9. weren't
10. weren't

Part D. Review

Practice 10, page 118

The following past tense verb forms are possible choices:

1. hiked
2. came, looked
3. gasped
4. loomed
5. ran
6. climbed
7. stretched
8. decorated
9. was
10. called
11. disappeared

Practice 11, page 118

The paragraph should be written:

(1) Above the office where I worked was a karate studio. (2) Every day as I went through my files, made out invoices, and wrote letters, I heard loud shrieks and crashes from the studio above me. (3) All day long, the walls trembled, the ceiling shook, and little pieces of plaster fell like snow onto my desk. (4) Sometimes, the noise did not bother me; other times, I wore earplugs. (5) If I was in a very bad mood, I stood on my desk and pounded out reggae rhythms on the ceiling with my shoe. (6) However, I did appreciate one thing. (7) The job taught me to concentrate, no matter what.

Chapter Review, page 119

The following past tense verb forms should be listed:

1. led
2. triumphed
3. began
4. postponed, financed, earned
5. came
6. moved, became
7. studied, lived
8. paid
9. graduated
10. completed
11. were
12. married
13. raised, worked
14. found
15. was
16. called
17. shared
18. offered, refused, was
19. struck, killed
20. drove
21. stepped
22. achieved
23. risked
24. established, lectured, continued
25. died

Chapter 10 The Past Participle in Action

Part B. Past Participles of Regular Verbs

Practice 1, page 123

The following past participles should be listed:

1. worked
2. boiled
3. hatched
4. congratulated
5. studied

6. scaled
7. asked
8. located
9. circled
10. signed

Practice 2, page 124

The following two-part verbs should be listed:

1. have wanted
2. have fulfilled
3. have used
4. has dropped
5. has shortened

6. have retained
7. has turned
8. has transformed
9. has renamed
10. have picked

Part C. Past Participles of Irregular Verbs

Practice 3, page 127

The following two-part verbs should be listed:

1. has risen
2. has sold
3. have sung
4. have fallen
5. has given

6. have thought
7. have kept
8. have forgotten
9. has frozen
10. have known

Practice 4, page 128

1. They have brought their Great Dane to the party.
2. T. J. has driven a city bus for two years.
3. She has chosen a Van Gogh poster for the hallway.
4. I have seen a white fox near the barn.
5. A tornado has torn through the shopping center.
6. Margo has become more self-confident.
7. Councilman Gomez has run a fair campaign.
8. The old barn has stood there for years.
9. Sam has read about the islands of Fiji.
10. Our conversations have been very helpful.

Practice 5, page 128

The following present and past tense verbs and past participles should be listed:

Present Tense (he, she, it)	Past Tense	Past Participle
knows	knew	known
catches	caught	caught
stops	stopped	stopped
breaks	broke	broken
reaches	reached	reached
brings	brought	brought
flies	flew	flown
falls	fell	fallen
feels	felt	felt
takes	took	taken
goes	went	gone

Practice 6, page 129

The following two-part verbs should be listed:

1. has broken
2. has established
3. have sold
5. has blazed
6. has received
8. have crossed

9. has come
11. has earned
12. have encouraged
14. has won
16. has become
17. have helped, have opened

Part D. Using the Present Perfect Tense

Practice 8, page 133

The following verbs should be circled:

1. loved
2. got
3. has invented
4. has lived and worked
5. has begun

6. has expanded
7. decided
8. created
9. said
10. have made

Practice 9, page 133

The following verb forms should be listed:

1. has spent
2. has accumulated
3. arrived, had
4. offered, opened
5. started

6. has gotten
7. contacted
8. has helped
9. has felt
10. has come

Part E. Using the Past Perfect Tense

Practice 10, page 135

The following two-part verbs should be listed:

1. has left
2. had left
3. have wanted
4. had wanted
5. had chosen

6. has chosen
7. has drunk
8. had drunk
9. had decided
10. has decided

Part F. Using the Passive Voice

Practice 11, page 136

The following verbs should be underlined and voices listed:

1. was born — P
2. enjoyed — A
3. defended — A
4. were charged — P
5. was arrested — P
6. gave — A
7. was imprisoned — P
8. did break — A
9. said — A
10. became — A
11. lined — A
12. was elected — P

Practice 12, page 137

The following verbs should be underlined, the subjects circled, and arrows drawn:

1. (The skaters) were applauded vigorously by the crowd.

2. (The corn) is picked fresh every morning.

3. (These flowered bowls) were imported from Mexico.

4. (Milos, my cat,) was ignored by the mouse.

5. (Hasty promises) are often broken.

6. (An antique train set) was sold at the auction.

7. (The speech) was memorized by both actors.

8. (Customers) are lured into the store by loud music and bright signs.

9. (Dutch) is spoken on Curaçao.

10. (Our quarrel) was quickly forgotten.

Practice 13, page 137

1. A small group of French doctors created Doctors Without Borders in 1971.
2. They provided excellent health care to people in poor or isolated regions.
3. Soon volunteer doctors and nurses from all over the world joined them.
4. Today the organization brings drugs and medical supplies to people in need.
5. Children in eighty countries receive vaccinations.
6. Volunteers restore crumbling hospitals and clinics.
7. The DWB staff also treats victims of wars.
8. The world gets information about humanitarian crises.
9. Each year, these traveling experts give the gifts of health and life to thousands.

Part G. Using Past Participles as Adjectives

Practice 14, page 139

The following linking verbs should be underlined and past participles circled:

1. is (guaranteed)
2. seems (qualified)
3. appears (delighted)
4. were (confused)
5. is (air-conditioned)
6. feels (appreciated)
7. gets (divorced)
8. were (thrilled)
9. feels (depressed)
10. Are (fried) (baked) (boiled)

Practice 15, page 140

The following past participles and sentences are possible answers:

1. A <u>worried</u> man checked his e-mail every few minutes.
2. Charlie's Angels could not find the <u>hidden</u> emeralds.
3. Please defrost these <u>frozen</u> muffins.
4. A <u>trained</u> nurse must give the blood transfusion.
5. Two <u>embarrassed</u> passengers searched for their train tickets.

Practice 16, page 140

The following past participles should be underlined and verb-tense corrections made:

          pleased
    (1) We are <u>please</u> to introduce three automobiles this year, each one <u>created</u> by our
experienced
<u>experience</u> team of engineers. (2) Our racy new sport model, the Hormone, is <u>guaranteed</u> to provide
           equipped   ***belted***
adventure on the road. (3) It comes <u>equip</u> with a powerful fuel-<u>injected</u> engine, steel-<u>belt</u> tires, and

orange flames <u>painted</u> across the hood. (4) Growing families will prefer the Sesame ST. (5) Blue
                      made
and modest on the outside, the Sesame ST's interior is <u>make</u> for parents and children. (6) Its

plastic upholstery is <u>printed</u> with yellow Big Bird designs. (7) Pop-out soda and hamburger
     preinstalled   ***programmed***
holders come <u>preinstall</u>, and the sound system is <u>program</u> for soft rock only, so your kids can't tune

in to grunge, hard rock, or rap stations. (8) For the budget-<u>minded</u> car shopper, we offer the
      equipped
Chintz. (9) It comes <u>equip</u> with a two-cylinder engine, steering wheel, and seats. (10) Recently, on
                      named
The Tonight Show with Jay Leno, the Chintz was <u>name</u> "the car that gives you less for less."

Practice 17, page 141

The following past participles should be underlined; the sentences are possible answers.

1. <u>dry-cleaned</u>   This dry-cleaned rug looks new.
2. <u>fallen</u>   He can bring up his fallen grades.
3. <u>sealed</u>   Harriet opened the sealed envelope.
4. <u>revised</u>   The revised weather forecast calls for sunshine.
5. <u>overpriced</u>   Do not buy these overpriced gold chains.

Practice 18, page 141

The following sentences should be written:

1. Your car was repaired.
2. The store looks closed.
3. My feelings are hurt.
4. The seats were filled.
5. She was relaxed.
6. You seem qualified for the job.
7. He was supposed to meet us.
8. They were used to hard work.
9. It is written in longhand.
10. You were expected at noon.

Chapter Review, page 142

The following past participle corrections should be made:

Three Ways to Be a Smarter Learner

(1) Once in a great while, a person is born with a photographic memory, allowing him or her
struggled
to memorize a lot of information with almost no effort. (2) However, most of us have ~~struggle~~ on

our own to find the best ways to learn. (3) We have stayed up all night studying. (4) We have
marked   *skilled*
~~mark~~ up our textbooks, highlighting and underlining like ~~skill~~ tattoo artists. (5) Maybe, in

frustration, we have even questioned our own intelligence. (6) Although everyone has his or her
made
own learning style, three techniques have ~~make~~ me and others better learners.
chosen
(7) The first technique is simple—sit at the front of the class! (8) A student who has ~~choose~~
involved
to sit up front is more likely to stay alert and ~~involve~~ than students at the back and sides. (9) By

sitting away from windows or talkative friends, many students discover that they take a greater

interest in the classroom subject and take better notes. (10) An extra benefit of sitting up front is
impressed
that teachers are often ~~impress~~ by students with whom they make eye contact, students whose

behavior says, "I care about this class."

(11) Second, make a smart friend. (12) During the first week of class, exchange phone numbers

with another front-row student. (13) You are looking for an intelligent, responsible classmate who
agreed
seems committed to learning—not for a pizza buddy or a date. (14) Students who have ~~agree~~ in
discussed
advance to help each other can call if they miss a class. (15) What was ~~discuss~~ that day?
assigned
(16) Was homework ~~assign~~ or a test announced? (17) Two students who "click" might want to

become study partners, meeting regularly to review material and prepare for tests.
sat   *paid*
(18) Third, ask questions. (19) The student who has ~~sit~~ up front, made a study friend, and ~~pay~~

close attention in class should not be worried about asking the professor questions. (20) Learning a
built
subject is like building a tower. (21) Each new level of understanding must be ~~build~~ solidly on the

level below. (22) If an important point or term is unclear, ask for help, in or after class.

increased

(23) Students who use these techniques will be rewarded with ~~increase~~ understanding and

pulled

better grades—even before they have ~~pull~~ out their pastel highlighters.

Maurice Jabbar, student

Chapter 11 Progressive Tenses (TO BE + –ING Verb Form)

Part A. Defining and Writing the Present Progressive Tense

Practice 1, page 145

The following helping verbs should be listed:

1. are
2. are
3. is
4. is
5. are

6. is
7. is
8. am
9. is
10. are

Practice 2, page 145

1. The telephone is ringing.
2. Dexter is wrestling with his math homework.
3. James and Judy are working in the emergency room.
4. I am keeping a journal of thoughts and observations.
5. We are polishing all our old tools.

Part B. Defining and Writing the Past Progressive Tense

Practice 3, page 146

The following helping verbs should be listed:

1. were
2. were
3. was
4. was
5. were

6. was
7. was
8. was
9. was
10. were

Practice 4, page 147

1. The two linebackers were growling at each other.
2. Leroy was examining his bank receipt.
3. We were watching the news.
4. Marsha was reading the *Wall Street Journal*.
5. He was painting like a professional artist.

Part C. Using the Progressive Tenses

Practice 5, page 148

The following verbs should be circled:

1. held
2. is driving
3. get
4. was thinking
5. eats

6. is eating
7. was frying, went
8. am studying
9. was sitting, discovered
10. sank

Part D. Avoiding Incomplete Progressives

Practice 6, page 149

The following Xs should be marked and present progressive and past progressive verbs listed:

	X		
1.	Fran and I watching the sunrise.	are	were
	X		
2.	You taking a computer course.	are	were
	X		
3.	A big log floating down the river.	is	was
	X		
4.	Her study skills improving.	are	were
	X		
5.	I trying to give up caffeine.	am	was
	X		
6.	Fights about money getting me down.	are	were
	X		
7.	Thick fog blanketing the city.	is	was
	X		
8.	That child reading already.	is	was
	X		
9.	Your pizza getting cold.	is	was
	X		
10.	They discussing the terms of the new contract.	are	were

Chapter Review, page 150

The following progressive verbs should be completed:

are

(1) Scientists studying the role of human genes in everything from eye color to intelligence to
∧

the tendency to get heart disease. (2) Recently, a map of every gene in the human body—three

are

billion elements in all—was completed by researchers of the Human Genome Project. (3) Scientists
∧

is

using this new information to find the genes that cause certain diseases. (4) Already, the map
∧

leading to cures and to other helpful discoveries, like finding bacteria that eat up oil spills and

are   *are*

then die. (5) On the other hand, ethical problems arising. (6) Some insurance companies refusing to
∧   ∧

insure healthy people who carry certain genes. (7) In the future, will employers be allowed to use

genetic tests the way some now use lie detectors or drug tests? (8) Will parents try to plan the

are

physical traits or talents of their babies? (9) Because of questions like these, some people calling
∧

genetic research a Pandora's box, not a magic bullet.

Chapter 12 Fixed-Form Helping Verbs and Verb Problems

Part A. Defining and Spotting the Fixed-Form Helping Verbs

Practice 1, page 151

The following fixed-form helping verbs should be listed:

1. can
2. must
3. will
4. might
5. may

6. can, will
7. should
8. may
9. should
10. may

Part B. Using the Fixed-Form Helping Verbs

Practice 2, page 152

The following main verb forms should be listed:

1. write
2. begin
3. visit
4. sleep
5. run

6. see
7. drizzle
8. go
9. study
10. be

Part C. Using CAN and COULD

Practice 3, page 154

The following present or past tense helping verbs should be listed:

1.	can	6.	can
2.	could	7.	can
3.	can	8.	could
4.	could	9.	could
5.	could	10.	can

Practice 4, page 154

The following present and past tense helping verbs should be circled:

1.	can	6.	could
2.	could	7.	can, could
3.	could	8.	could
4.	can	9.	could
5.	can	10.	can

Part D. Using WILL and WOULD

Practice 6, page 155

The following present and past tense helping verbs should be listed:

1.	will	6.	would
2.	would	7.	will
3.	would	8.	will
4.	will	9.	will
5.	will	10.	would

Practice 7, page 155

The following present and past tense helping verbs should be circled:

1.	will	6.	would
2.	will	7.	will
3.	would	8.	would
4.	would	9.	will
5.	would	10.	would

Part E. Writing Infinitives

Practice 8, page 156

The following infinitives should be listed:

1. to leave
2. to run
3. to get

4. to think
5. to buy, to give

Practice 9, page 157

The following infinitives are possible choices:

1. to dance
2. to skate
3. to meet

4. to become
5. to learn to knit

Part F. Revising Double Negatives

Practice 10, page 158

The following sentences are possible choices:

1. I can hardly wait for Christmas vacation.
2. Ms. Chandro has never been to Los Angeles before.
3. Fido was so excited that he could scarcely sit still.
4. Nat won't talk to anybody until he's finished studying.
5. Yesterday's newspaper didn't contain any ads for large-screen television sets.
6. Alice doesn't have a bathing suit with her.
7. If Harold were smart, he wouldn't answer anyone in that tone of voice.
8. Kylie claimed that she had never been to a rodeo before.
9. Some days, I can't seem to do anything right.
10. Umberto searched, but he couldn't find his gold bow tie anywhere.

Chapter Review, page 160

The following corrections should be made:

Man of Honor

(1) According to public opinion polls, the most influential Hispanic American in the country
could
is Edward James Olmos. (2) Olmos is someone who ~~couldn't~~ never be happy promoting only
set
himself. (3) He has tried to ~~setting~~ an example for others through his choice of movie roles.
any
(4) Olmos decided early that he would not take ~~no~~ parts in *Rambo*- and *Terminator*-style movies

just to get rich. (5) Instead, he wanted his life work to be something that he and his descendants
would
~~will~~ be proud of.

(6) As a result, his film projects have included *American Me*, an examination of gang members

and life in prison. (7) Young people have told him that this film persuaded them that they

should not have ~~nothing~~ *anything* to do with gangs. (8) Olmos is also famous for his portrayal of teacher

Jaime Escalante in *Stand and Deliver*. (9) Other projects, from an anti–domestic violence

documentary to a film about Brazilian political activist Chico Mendes called *The Burning Season*,

aimed to ~~educating~~ *educate* the public.

(10) Olmos also hopes that he ~~would~~ *will* change lives through his community activism. (11) He

gives antidrug speeches. (12) In addition, Olmos visits public schools and promotes projects that

help Latinos. (13) For example, he cofounded and now codirects the Los Angeles Latino

International Film Festival. (14) The actor also supports the Latino Book and Family Festival and

oversees Latino Public Broadcasting. (15) Olmos knows from experience that one person ~~could~~ *can* make

a difference.

Unit 3 Review

Transforming, page 162

The following corrections should be made:

A. (1) The race is about to begin. (2) ~~My~~ *Her* heart pounds as ~~I peel~~ *she peels* off ~~my~~ *her* sweatpants and jacket
and ~~drop~~ *drops* them on the grass. (3) ~~I step~~ *She steps* onto the new, all-weather track and ~~enter my~~ *enters her* assigned lane.
(4) Next, ~~I check my~~ *she checks her* track shoes for loose laces. (5) By now, the athletes around ~~me~~ *her* are stretching
backwards, forwards, and sideways. (6) ~~I extend~~ *She extends* one leg, then the other, and ~~bend~~ *bends* low, giving ~~my~~ *her*
hamstrings a final stretch. (7) Although ~~I~~ *she* never ~~come~~ *comes* eye to eye with ~~my~~ *her* opponents, ~~I feel~~ *she feels* their
readiness as they exhale loudly. (8) Their energy charges the air like electricity. (9) ~~I plant my~~ *She plants her*
feet in the blocks. (10) Off to one side, a coach starts to speak. (11) ~~My~~ *Her* mind is flashing. (12) How
will ~~my~~ *her* opponents kick off? (13) How will they start? (14) The seconds swell, thick and

dreamlike. (15) The gun sounds.

Sheila Grant, student

                was   *slept*

B. (1) It ~~is~~ the morning of April 18, 1906. (2) Alfred Hunt ~~sleeps~~ peacefully in the

                                          shook

Palace Hotel in San Francisco. (3) At 5:12, a violent jolt suddenly ~~shakes~~ his room

sent   *lasted*

and ~~sends~~ him rolling from bed. (4) The shaking ~~lasts~~ for forty-five seconds. (5) During

                    staggered   *rocked*

the calm of the next ten seconds, Hunt ~~staggers~~ to the window. (6) Another tremor ~~rocks~~

                        watched   *looked*

the city for twenty-five more seconds. (7) Hunt ~~watches~~ in terror. (8) The whole city ~~looks~~ like

                    reeled   *tumbled*   *broke*   *started*

breaking waves. (9) Buildings ~~reel~~ and ~~tumble~~ to the ground. (10) Then fires ~~break~~ out and ~~start~~ to

                    dressed, threw   *ran*

spread. (11) Hunt quickly ~~dresses, throws~~ open his door, and ~~runs~~ downstairs into the street.

                    blocked   *carried*

(12) Crowds of rushing people ~~block~~ his path. (13) Some people ~~carry~~ screaming children while

struggled   *took*

others ~~struggle~~ under loads of furniture and other valuable objects. (14) It ~~takes~~ Hunt four hours to

                                                        would

push through the four blocks from his hotel to the safety of the Oakland ferry. (15) Later, he ~~will~~

                                    had   *had*

learn that the great San Francisco earthquake ~~has~~ destroyed 520 city blocks and ~~has~~ killed more

than seven hundred people.

Proofreading, page 163

The following corrections should be made:

Protector of the Chimps

            done

(1) Jane Goodall has <u>did</u> more than anyone else to understand the lives of chimpanzees.

(2) Always an animal lover, Goodall was too poor to go to college to study animals. (3) She worked

                                                                 went

as a waitress until the age of twenty-five. (4) Then she fulfilled a lifelong dream and <u>gone</u> to East

Africa. (5) There she was thrilled by the beauty of the land and the wild animals.

                met   *recognized*

(6) In Africa, she <u>meet</u> Louis Leakey, a famous naturalist. (7) Leakey <u>recognize</u> Goodall's

curiosity, energy, and passion for the natural world. (8) He hired her for a six-month study of the

wild chimpanzees in a national park in Tanzania. (9) Despite malaria, primitive living

conditions, and hostile wildlife, Goodall followed the activities of a group of chimps in the

                    watched

Gombe forest. (10) For months, she <u>watch</u> the chimps through binoculars. (11) She moved closer

            became

and closer until she eventually <u>become</u> part of their lives. (12) Goodall named the chimps and

were
recorded their daily activities. (13) She learned that chimps <u>was</u> capable of feeling happiness,

anger, and pain. (14) They formed complex societies with leaders, politics, and tribal wars.

was
(15) One of her most important discoveries <u>were</u> that chimps made and used tools. (16) Goodall

expected to stay in Gombe for six months; instead she studied the chimps there for almost forty

led
years. (17) Her studies <u>lead</u> to a totally new understanding of chimps, and she became world

famous.

attended
(18) However, her life changed completely in 1986. (19) She <u>attend</u> a conference in Chicago,

where she heard horrible stories about the fate of chimps outside Gombe. (20) She learned about

the destruction of the forests and the wildlife of Africa. (21) From that day on, Goodall

given
committed herself to education and conservation. (22) Since then, she has traveled, lectured, <u>gave</u>

interviews, and met with people. (23) She established both the Jane Goodall Institute and a young

carried
people's group, Roots & Shoots. (24) These worldwide organizations have already <u>carry</u> out many

important conservation and educational projects. (25) The author of remarkable books and the

known
subject of inspiring television specials, Jane Goodall is <u>knowed</u> for her total commitment to chimps

and to a healthy natural world.

Unit 3 Writers' Workshop, page 164

1.   Y   Y
        Y   Y
6. No errors

UNIT 4
Joining Ideas Together

Chapter 13 Coordination

Practice 1, page 169

The following corrections should be made:

1. Desert, for
2. City, yet/but
3. Festival, for
4. theme, and/so
5. theme, so
6. festival, yet/but
7. allowed, nor
8. group, for
9. beach, but/yet
10. party, or

Practice 2, page 170

1. Babies need constant supervision, so you should never leave them by themselves.
2. I will write my essay at home tonight, or I will write it tomorrow in the computer lab.
3. In the 1840s, American women began to fight for the right to vote, yet they did not win that right until 1920.
4. Rico overcame his disappointment, and he decided to try again.
5. They are the best Ping-Pong players on the block, but they can't beat my cousin from Cleveland.
6. The ancient Chinese valued peaches, for they believed that eating peaches made a person immortal.

Practice 3, page 170

The following answers are possible choices:

1. I try not to get upset.
2. his English is quite good.
3. now he's a widower.
4. it allows me to drive to the country on weekends.
5. I hate the repair bills.

Chapter Review, page 172

The following corrections are possible choices:

(1) In 1929, Alice Orr answered a want ad for bronco riders for a Wild West show. (2) She was

immediately, and her

hired ~~immediately.~~ (3) ~~Her~~ new job launched a remarkable career. (4) Orr became an international

event, but her

rodeo star. (5) She was an expert in every rodeo ~~event.~~ (6) ~~Her~~ specialty was saddle bronc riding.

rodeos, yet

(7) That tough competition has since been dropped from women's ~~rodeos.~~ (8) Orr won four world

competitors, so

championships in it. (9) Orr was also concerned about working conditions for rodeo ~~competitors.~~

she

(10) ~~She~~ helped establish a professional rodeo association. (11) In the 1940s, Orr and her husband

themselves, and she

put on rodeos ~~themselves.~~ (12) ~~She~~ would demonstrate her world-famous saddle bronc riding.

fifties, but she

(13) Orr retired from rodeos in her ~~fifties.~~ (14) ~~She~~ did movie stunt work until she was eighty.

(15) When Alice Orr died in 1995 at the age of 93, many people still remembered her as queen of

the bronco riders.

Chapter 14 Subordination

Part A. Defining and Using Subordinating Conjunctions

Practice 1, page 174

The following answers are possible choices:

1. While
2. Although
3. When
4. because
5. whereas
6. after
7. before
8. whenever
9. until
10. so that
11. Whenever
12. As
13. since
14. because
15. if

Practice 2, page 175

The following answers are possible choices:

1. the college hired a new food manager.
2. they often attend local games.
3. the store won't refund his money,
4. Noah was ironing clothes.
5. you write that article,

Part B. Punctuating Subordinating Conjunctions

Practice 3, page 176

The following answers should be listed:

1.	hungry,	9.	C
2.	1954,	10.	C
3.	hamburgers,	11.	i f
4.	C	12.	C
5.	advantages,	13.	grams,
6.	booming,	14.	delicious,
7.	day,	15.	food,
8.	cheese,		

Practice 4, page 177

The following sentences are possible answers:

1. When young couples in India marry, the ceremony may last for days.
    The ceremony may last for days when young couples in India marry.

2. After the wedding takes place at the bride's home, everyone travels to the groom's home for more celebrating.
    Everyone travels to the groom's home for more celebrating after the wedding takes place at the bride's home.

3. Because ducks mate for life, they are often included in Korean wedding processions.
    Ducks are often included in Korean wedding processions because they mate for life.

4. Whereas Iroquois brides gave grain to their mothers-in-law, mothers-in-law gave meat to the brides.
    Iroquois brides gave grain to their mothers-in-law whereas mothers-in-law gave meat to the brides.

5. When the food was exchanged, the bride and groom were considered married.
    The bride and groom were considered married when the food was exchanged.

6. Until the tradition went out of style, Finnish brides and grooms used to exchange wreaths.
    Finnish brides and grooms used to exchange wreaths until the tradition went out of style.

7. Unless the bride, groom, and bridal party dance special dances, a Zulu wedding is not complete.
    A Zulu wedding is not complete unless the bride, groom, and bridal party dance special dances.

8. As the bride dances wildly and gloriously, she stabs at imaginary enemies with a knife.
    The bride stabs at imaginary enemies with a knife as she dances wildly and gloriously.

9. Although the wedding ring is a very old symbol, the elaborate wedding cake is even older.
    The wedding ring is a very old symbol although the elaborate wedding cake is even older.

10. Whereas the ring symbolizes the oneness of the new couple, the cake represents fertility.
     The cake represents fertility whereas the ring symbolizes the oneness of the new couple.

Chapter Review, page 180

The following sentences are possible answers:

(1) Jacob Lawrence was a great American painter, a powerful teller of stories on canvas.
After young   *1930, he*
(2) ~~Young~~ Jacob joined his mother in Harlem in ~~1930.~~ (3) ~~He~~ began to paint the people around him.
                          Harlem because the
(4) Luckily, he found excellent art classes in ~~Harlem.~~ (5) ~~The~~ big art academies often excluded
      When he   *twenty-three, he*
blacks then. (6) ~~He~~ was only ~~twenty-three.~~ (7) ~~He~~ gained fame for his sixty-picture *Migration*
                                      paintings although no
Series. (8) A New York gallery displayed these ~~paintings.~~ (9) ~~No~~ major commercial gallery had

showcased an African-American artist before. (10) The *Migration Series* depicts southern blacks

journeying north to find work after World War I. (11) The paintings show people searching for a
       While   *endured, he*
better life. (12) Lawrence's work portrays the poverty and prejudice the migrants ~~endured.~~ (13) ~~He~~
         ^

also wanted viewers of his work "to experience the beauty of life." (14) During his long career,

Lawrence painted many more energetic canvases and series. (15) His work reminds us that we are
      migrants because we
all ~~migrants.~~ (16) ~~We~~ are always on the move. (17) We are seeking something more.

Chapter 15 Avoiding Run-Ons and Comma Splices

Practice 1, page 183

The following corrections are possible choices:

                                                       abuse, but
1. Many famous people today have struggled with alcoholism or drug ~~abuse~~ some have   <u>RO</u>

    overcome these problems.
                                                       recovery because
2. Often politicians, athletes, and actors hide their addiction and their ~~recovery,~~ they   <u>CS</u>

    do not want to risk ruining their careers.

3. Other celebrities choose to go public in their battles with alcohol or drugs.   <u>C</u>
                                                        so
4. A few feel that their struggles may help others, they want to act as positive role   <u>CS</u>
                                            ^
    models.

5. One such person was Betty Ford, a former First ~~Lady with~~ **Lady. With** her family's help, she   RO

   became sober at age sixty.

6. ~~Her~~ **Because her** recovery was ~~successful~~ **successful,** she agreed to help several friends create a treatment   RO

   center in Rancho Mirage, California.

7. At the Betty Ford Center, celebrities like Liz Taylor and Kelsey Grammer as well as   C

   everyday people receive support for their new way of life.

8. Treatment centers now exist around the country, **for** the problem of addiction seems to be   CS
                                                    ∧
   increasing, especially among the young.

9. For example, Drew Barrymore was famous at age six for her role in the film *E.T.*, **but** by   CS
                                                                                     ∧
   age nine she was addicted to drugs and alcohol.

10. Forced her into rehab at age thirteen, Drew was able to get her acting career back on   C

    track.

11. ~~Actors~~ **Although actors** Charlie Sheen, Matthew Perry, and Ben Affleck likewise developed   RO
    ~~addictions~~ **addictions,** getting treatment helped them stay on top of their profession.

12. Football legend Lawrence Taylor is one of many athletes who have gone through   CS
    detox, **but** he claims that at last he has turned his life around.
          ∧

13. Stardom seems to invite the risk of addiction; the Musicians' Assistance Program has   C

    helped over 1,500 rock stars get straight.

14. Alcohol and drugs might seem glamorous, especially to the young, **yet** they can destroy   CS
                                                                      ∧
    relationships, careers, and self-esteem.

15. ~~Millions~~ **While millions** of Americans are affected, when someone returns from addiction, his or   CS

    her triumph can encourage others to seek help.

Practice 2, page 184

The following sentences are possible choices:

1. (a) For instance, when you want to purchase a car, you may walk up to an outdoor booth.
   (b) For instance, you want to purchase a car, so you may walk up to an outdoor booth.
2. (a) After you select the options on a computer screen, you press an order entry key.
   (b) You select the options on a computer screen, and you press an order entry key.
3. (a) A factory assembles your car, and it is later delivered to your local dealer.
   (b) A factory assembles your car. It is later delivered to your local dealer.
4. (a) When you go to a store to buy jeans, none are on the shelf.
   (b) You go to a store to buy jeans, but none are on the shelf.
5. (a) Instead, as you look at different styles onscreen, you make your choice.
   (b) Instead, you look at different styles onscreen, and you make your choice.
6. (a) Although taking measurements is not new, now they can be taken by a three-dimensional camera.
   (b) Taking measurements is not new, but now they can be taken by a three-dimensional camera.
7. (a) Because your measurements have been taken electronically, your jeans will fit perfectly.
   (b) Your measurements have been taken electronically, so your jeans will fit perfectly.
8. (a) Your selection and measurements are transmitted to a factory. Your jeans are made to order.
   (b) Your selection and measurements are transmitted to a factory, and your jeans are made to order.
9. (a) If you want someone to experiment with changing your hairstyle, a computer screen will show you with long, short, or differently colored hair.
   (b) You want to experiment with changing your hairstyle. A computer screen will show you with long, short, or differently colored hair.
10. (a) Although you can leave the way you came in, you can leave with a new look.
    (b) You can leave the way you came in, or you can leave with a new look.

Chapter Review, page 186

The following corrections are possible choices:

A. (1) Skateboarder Tony Hawk has not only dramatically changed his sport, **but** he has **also** contributed to the popularity of all extreme sports. (2) The wholesome Hawk is responsible for cleaning up skateboarding's early reputation as the pastime of rebels and ~~hoodlums now~~ **hoodlums. Now** it's an acceptable, mainstream activity. (3) Hawk is also famous for defying the laws of physics to create amazing new aerial acrobatics. (4) In 1999, at the age of thirty-one, he was the first skater ever to complete a ~~900, this~~ **900. This** is a 360-degree spin done two-and-a-half times in mid-air. (5) As a result, he is called "the Michael Jordan of skateboarding." (6) Today, although he has retired from competition, he performs in exhibitions all over the ~~country~~ **country, and** surveys of young people reveal that he is more popular than Shaquille O'Neal or Tiger Woods. (7) Hawk's fame has created a

huge interest in skateboarding. (8) In 2001, 8.2 million Americans under the age of eighteen played
but
baseball, ∧ 10.6 million skateboarded. (9) Today, these young athletes roll into skate parks that

have sprung up all over the country, thanks to Hawk's influence.
                                                           year. It
     B. (1) Nearly one million people traveled to Graceland last ~~year it~~ is the most visited home

in America except for the White House. (2) In case you didn't know, Graceland was the home of
                                   Presley. He
rock-and-roll legend Elvis ~~Presley he~~ bought it in 1957 at the age of twenty-two when he suddenly

became rich and famous. (3) It was opened to the public in 1982, five years after Elvis died there.
                                                                    so
(4) The eighteen-room Memphis mansion was Elvis's home for twenty years, ∧ visitors can see what

was considered luxury living in the 1960s and 1970s. (5) Vinyl beanbag chairs, mirrored ceilings,

and shag carpeting were high fashion then. (6) However, many visitors travel to the singer's

home to honor the man rather than to see the house. (7) For some, a trip to Graceland has become a
            experience. During
spiritual ~~experience during~~ Elvis Presley's "Death Week," tens of thousands arrive from all over

the world to honor their idol.

     C. (1) What do you do every night before you go to sleep and every morning when you wake
                                  but
up? (2) You probably brush your teeth, ∧ most people in the United States did not start brushing

their teeth until after the 1850s. (3) People living in the nineteenth century did not have
toothpaste.
~~toothpaste,~~ Dr. Washington Wentworth Sheffield developed a tooth-cleaning substance, which

soon became widely available. (4) With the help of his son, this Connecticut dentist changed our
                          toothpaste. It
daily habits by making the first ~~toothpaste it~~ was called Dr. Sheffield's Creme Dentifrice.
Because the
(5) ~~The~~ product was not marketed cleverly enough, the idea of using toothpaste caught on slowly.
                            tubes, and
(6) Then toothpaste was put into tin ~~tubes~~ everyone wanted to try this new product. (7) Think of
                               toothpaste, and
life without tubes of mint-flavored ~~toothpaste~~ then thank Dr. Sheffield for his idea.
                                                     because
     D. (1) The first semester of college is difficult for many students ∧ they must take on many new

responsibilities. (2) For instance, they must create their own schedules. (3) New students get to
            courses. In
select their ~~courses in~~ addition, they have to decide when they will take them. (4) Students also

textbooks. Colleges

must purchase their own ~~textbooks, colleges~~ do not distribute textbooks each term as high schools

end, yet

do. (5) No bells ring to announce when classes begin and ~~end~~ students are supposed to arrive on time.

roll, for

(6) Furthermore, many professors do not call the ~~roll~~ they expect students to attend classes

regularly and know the assignments. (7) Above all, new students must be self-disciplined. (8) No

help.

one stands over them telling them to do their homework or to visit the writing lab for extra ~~help,~~

They

~~they~~ must balance the temptation to have fun and the desire to build a successful future.

E. (1) Languages are disappearing in countries on every continent. (2) North America has two

but

hundred Native American languages, only about fifty now have more than a thousand speakers.

(3) The Celtic languages of northwest Europe also have been declining for many generations.

(4) However, the death of languages is most noticeable in isolated communities in Asia and

community. Sometimes

Australia. (5) A different language is spoken in each tiny ~~community sometimes~~ only ten people

speak it.

(6) In such small communities, a whole language can die if one village perishes.

When   *1960s,*

(7) Westerners explored a rain forest in Venezuela in the 1960s they carried a flu virus into a tiny

and

community. (8) The virus killed all the villagers, their language disappeared with them.

(9) However, most languages fade out when a smaller community comes into close contact with a

one. People

larger, more powerful ~~one, people~~ begin to use the "more important" language. (10) A language

that gives better access to education, jobs, and new technology usually prevails over a native

mother tongue.

(11) According to scholars who study languages, almost half of the world's 6,500 languages

languages because

are in danger of extinction. (12) That statistic represents more than the loss of specific ~~languages,~~

every language represents a way of looking at the world. (13) Whenever a language disappears,

we lose a unique point of view. (14) No other language can really take its place.

Chapter 16 Semicolons and Conjunctive Adverbs

Part A. Defining and Using Semicolons

Practice 1, page 190

The following answers are possible choices:

1. ; both of them ran in opposite directions.
2. ; it was filled with canvases and old magazines for collage images.
3. ; I have it programmed into my phone.
4. ; my coat was not where I had left it.
5. ; her second one has an automatic transmission.

Practice 2, page 191

The following sentences should be checked and completed:

2.   The library has installed new computers; we can find information faster now.
4.   She suddenly started to laugh; her dog had switched on the light.
5.   My answer is simple; I will not go.
6.   I cannot find my car keys; I have looked everywhere.
7.   The rain poured down in buckets; everyone left the stands.
10. Because you understand, I feel better; I am ready to try again.

Practice 3, page 192

The following corrections should be made:

(1) The Swiss Army knife is carried in the pockets and purses of millions of travelers,

campers, and just plain folks. (2) Numerous useful gadgets are folded into its famous red handle;
these
~~These~~ include knife blades, tweezers, scissors, toothpick, screwdriver, bottle opener, fish scaler,

tools,
and magnifying glass. (3) Because the knife contains many ~~tools;~~ it is also carried by explorers,

mountain climbers, and astronauts. (4) Lives have been saved by the Swiss Army knife. (5) It once
it
opened the iced-up oxygen system of someone climbing Mount Everest; ~~It~~ saved the lives of

scientists stranded on an island who used the tiny saw on the knife to cut branches for a fire.
1891 and
(6) The handy Swiss Army knife was created for Swiss soldiers in ~~1891; and~~ soon became popular
colors; many
all over the world. (7) It comes in many models and ~~colors many~~ people prefer the classic original.

(8) The Swiss Army knife deserves its reputation for beautiful design and usefulness; a red one is on

permanent display in New York's famous Museum of Modern Art.

Part B. Defining and Using Conjunctive Adverbs

Practice 4, page 194

The following answers are possible choices:

1. Uncle Sid pole-vaulted over the fence.
2. she sometimes offends people.
3. I won't wear the ten-gallon hat.
4. his little son might not be so polite.
5. she couldn't find time to take the training course for volunteers.
6. she had her coat and a tennis racket under her arm.
7. I will take time to shoot some baskets.
8. I record my mileage every time I fill the gas tank.

Part C. Punctuating Conjunctive Adverbs

Practice 5, page 194

The following corrections should be made:

1. Many people think that art is serious rather than ~~fun however~~ **fun; however,** they might change their

   minds if they could see a Cow Parade.

2. For this public art event, a city's artists decorate identical, life-size sculptures of ~~cows~~ **cows;**
   consequently, ~~consequently~~ each cow becomes a humorous artistic work.

3. In the Chicago and New York Cow Parades, the finished art objects were anything but dull
   and ~~reserved instead~~ **reserved; instead,** they were wildly creative.

4. Each artist picked a character or idea to ~~portray furthermore;~~ **portray; furthermore,** he or she gave that special

   bovine a fitting name.

5. For example, one cow was painted with stars and stripes to resemble our country's ~~flag~~ **flag;**
   consequently, ~~consequently~~ its name was "Americow the Beautiful."

6. Dark-eyed "Cowpatra" was decorated like the Queen of the ~~Nile meanwhile~~ **Nile; meanwhile,** "Moozart"

   wore the red velvet coat and white wig of that famous composer.

7. "Prima Cowlerina" posed in a pink tutu and four toe shoes, and "Cownt Dracula" had ~~fangs~~ **fangs;**
   therefore, ~~therefore~~ even blasé city dwellers paused to admire them.

8. Many cows were decorated with a famous work of ~~art consequently~~ *art; consequently,* they had names like

    "Picowso," "Mootisse," or "Vincent Van Cogh."

9. People seem to love meeting a plaster cow dressed in hip-hop clothing or covered with
    street; meanwhile,
    gumdrops on a city ~~street meanwhile~~ urban work and play can go on as usual.

    charity; therefore,
10. Each event concludes with an auction of the cows to benefit ~~charity therefore~~ a Cow Parade

    not only brings art to the public but also raises money for a good cause.

Practice 6, page 196

The following sentences are possible answers:

1. Marilyn fell asleep on the train; therefore, she missed her stop.
2. Last night Channel 20 televised a special about gorillas; however, I did not get home in time to see it.
3. Roberta writes to her nephew every month; furthermore, she sends a gift with every letter.
4. It takes me almost an hour to get to school each morning; nevertheless, the scenery makes the drive a pleasure.
5. Luke missed work on Monday; consequently, he did not proofread the quarterly report.

Chapter Review, page 198

The following corrections should be made:

(1) Perhaps you have seen a sleek circular symbol consisting of two connected teardrop

shapes, one white and one black. (2) This is the Chinese symbols of Yin Yang. (3) According to
opposites; consequently,
ancient Chinese philosophy, we live in a world of ~~opposites consequently~~ the world contains

female and male, dark and light, cold and hot, yin and yang. (4) Yin and yang represent
forces; however,
contrasting life ~~forces however~~ the symbol shows us a harmony of opposites that underlies the

universe. (5) On the one hand, yin is any force that is feminine, soft, receptive, hidden, cool, and
dark; thus,
~~dark, thus;~~ the dark part of the symbol represents yin. (6) Yang, on the other hand, describes any
light;
force that is masculine, hard, aggressive, open, hot, and ~~light,~~ therefore, the light part of the

symbol represents yang. (7) However, the Yin Yang symbol also contains a dot of black in the white area and a dot of white in the black area. (8) These dots remind us that nothing is simply black or ~~white~~ *white;* everything contains an element of the opposing force. (9) For example, all people are a mix of yin and yang qualities, whatever their gender. (10) The whole symbol seems to say that we know pleasure because we have felt pain, beauty because we have seen ugliness, and love because we have known its opposite.

Chapter 17 Relative Pronouns

Part A. Defining and Using Relative Pronouns

Practice 1, page 200

1. My uncle, who was a state champion, is giving me diving lessons.
2. Our marriage ceremony, which was quick and sweet, made our nervous parents happy.
3. The manatee is a sea mammal that lives along the Florida coast.
4. Donna bought a new backpack that has thickly padded straps.
5. This walking tour, which has thirty-two stops, is a challenge to complete.
6. Hockey, which is a fast-moving game, often becomes violent.
7. Andrew Jackson, who was born in South Carolina, was the seventh U.S. president.
8. At the beach, I always use sunscreen, which prevents burns and lessens the danger of skin cancer.

Part B. Punctuating Ideas Introduced by WHO, WHICH, or THAT

Practice 2, page 202

1. C
2. C
3. C
4. anaconda, world,
5. watch, date
6. Carol, attendant,
7. Upton, students,
8. C

Practice 3, page 202

The following answers are possible choices:

1. doesn't even like animals
2. works as a team
3. promise too much
4. lists all of Shakespeare's history plays
5. has wonderful restaurants
6. wants to be a pilot
7. have bargain basements
8. manufactures sportswear

Chapter Review, page 204

The following errors should be corrected:

Airmen,

(1) Charles Anderson is best known as the trainer of the Tuskegee ~~Airmen~~ who were the first

African-American combat pilots. (2) During a time when African Americans were prevented from

becoming pilots, Anderson was fascinated by planes. (3) He learned about flying from books. (4) At

plane, which

age twenty-two, he bought a used ~~plane which~~, became his teacher. (5) Eventually he met

someone

~~someone,~~ who helped him become an expert flyer. (6) Battling against discrimination, Anderson

became the first African American to earn an air transport pilot's license. (7) He and another pilot

made the first round-trip flight across America by black Americans. (8) In 1939, Anderson started

a civilian pilot training program at Tuskegee Institute in Alabama. (9) One day Eleanor

who   *time,*

Roosevelt, ~~which~~ was First Lady at the ~~time~~ insisted on flying with him. (10) Soon afterward,

Anderson,

Tuskegee Institute was chosen by the Army Air Corps for a special program. (11) ~~Anderson~~ who

instructor,

was chief flight ~~instructor~~ gave America's first African-American World War II pilots their

heroism,

initial training. (12) During the war, the Tuskegee Airmen showed great skill and ~~heroism~~ which

were later recognized by an extraordinary number of honors and awards.

Chapter 18 -ING Modifiers

Part A. Using -ING Modifiers

Practice 1, page 205

1. Searching for change, Kyla found her lost earring.

2. Working all evening, the children completed the jigsaw puzzle.

3. Hiking cross-country, they made many new friends.

4. Visiting Santa Fe, she decided to move there.

5. Loading your camera, you spot a grease mark on the lens.

6. Mumbling to himself, Seth named the fifty states.

7. Pounding his gavel, Judge Smithers called a recess.

8. Lifting huge rocks and cementing them in place, the masons built the wall carefully.

Part B. Avoiding Confusing Modifiers

Practice 2, page 207

1. Biking and walking daily, Cheryl cut her commuting costs.
2. Professor Fernandez spotted a monkey leaping from tree to tree.
3. Painting for three hours straight, Theresa finished the bathroom and the hallway.
4. Playing soccer in the schoolyard, my son spotted our dog.
5. Tonya discovered her calculus textbook lying in the driveway.

Chapter Review, page 208

The following errors should be corrected:

(1) What happened in the shed behind Patrick O'Leary's house to start the Great Chicago Fire of 1871? (2) No one knows for sure. (3) ~~Smoking in the shed, some~~ *Some* people say the fire was started by careless ~~boys.~~ *boys smoking in the shed.* (4) In another story, poker-playing youngsters accidentally kicked over an oil lamp. (5) However, the blame usually is placed on Mrs. O'Leary's cow. (6) At 8:45 p.m., swinging a lantern at her ~~side~~ *side,* Mrs. O'Leary went out to milk the unruly cow. (7) ~~The~~ cow tipped the ~~lantern switching its tail.~~ *Switching its tail, the lantern.* (8) Recalling the ~~incident Mrs.~~ *incident, Mrs.* Nellie Hayes branded the cow theory "nonsense." (9) In fact, she said that the O'Learys' neighbors were having a party on the hot night of October 7. (10) Looking for some fresh ~~milk~~ *milk,* a thirsty guest walked into the shed and dropped a lighted candle along the way. (11) Whatever happened, the fire was the greatest calamity of nineteenth-century America. (12) Killing three hundred people and destroying more than three square miles of ~~buildings it~~ *buildings, it* left ninety thousand people homeless.

Unit 4 Review

Proofreading, page 211

The following errors should be corrected:

Managing Time in College

(1) When I started college, time was a problem. (2) I was always desperately reading an assignment just before class or racing to get to work on time. (3) The stress became too much. (4) It took a ~~while~~ *while, but* now I know how to manage my time. (5) The secret of my success is flexible planning.

(6) At the beginning of each semester, I mark a calendar with all the due dates for the ~~term~~ *term.* *These* ~~these~~ include deadlines for assignments, papers, and tests. (7) I also write in social events and *obligations; therefore,* ~~obligations, therefore;~~ I know at a glance when I need extra time during the next few months.

(8) Next, I make out a model weekly study schedule. (9) First, I block in the hours when I have to sleep, eat, work, go to class, and tend to my ~~family then~~ *family. Then* I decide what time I will devote to study and relaxation. (10) Finally, I fill in the times I will study each subject, making sure I plan at least one hour of study time for each hour of class time. (11) Generally, I plan some time just before or after a ~~class that~~ *class. That* way I can prepare for a class or review my notes right after a lecture.

(12) In reality, I don't follow this schedule ~~rigidly,~~ *rigidly;* I vary it according to the demands of the week and day. (13) In addition, I spend more time on my harder subjects and less time on the easy ones. (14) I also try to study my harder subjects in the ~~morning,~~ *morning* when I am most awake.

(15) I find that by setting up a model schedule but keeping it flexible, I can accomplish all I have to do with little worry. (16) This system may not help ~~everyone,~~ *everyone; however,* it has certainly worked for me.

Jesse Rose, student

Combining, page 212

The following answers are possible choices:

1. Although the tide had not yet come in, we went swimming.
   The tide had not yet come in, but we went swimming.
2. Michael enjoys drinking coffee, yet he needs to limit his caffeine intake.
   Michael enjoys drinking coffee; nevertheless, he needs to limit his caffeine intake.
3. Alexis plays the trumpet very well, and she hopes to have her own band someday.
   Alexis plays the trumpet very well; furthermore, she hopes to have her own band someday.
4. Because the lecture starts in five minutes, we had better get to our seats.
   The lecture starts in five minutes, so we had better get to our seats.
5. Although he knows how to make money, he doesn't want to start another company.
   He knows how to make money; however, he doesn't want to start another company.

Revising, page 213

The following errors should be corrected:

(1) You may be ~~young.~~ *young, but you* (2) ~~You~~ are never too young to save money. (3) Save as much as you ~~can.~~ *can,*
(4) ~~Start~~ *and start* as early as you can. (5) Invest your money well. (6) Compound interest earns money on your ~~investment.~~ *investment; moreover, it* (7) ~~It~~ also earns money on the interest you earn.

(8) Start investing at an early ~~age.~~ *age; you* (9) ~~You~~ will see amazing results. (10) Perhaps you'd like

to have a million dollars by the age of sixty-five. (11) Look at the difference in the money you

would have to put away, depending on the age at which you get started. (12) ~~You~~ *If you* start at age

~~twenty.~~ *twenty, you* (13) ~~You~~ would need to invest $1,391 a year to reach your goal. (14) You could start at age

~~thirty.~~ *thirty, but you* (15) ~~You~~ would then need to invest $3,690 a year. (16) ~~You~~ *If you* wait until age ~~forty.~~ *forty, you* (17) ~~You~~

would need to invest $10,168 a year. (18) Starting at age fifty is not too ~~late.~~ *late; however, you* (19) ~~You~~ would have

to save $31,474 a year to reach your goal. (20) You can see the advantage of starting at a young age.

(21) We can look at the power of compound interest from another perspective. (22) Let's

imagine that you've saved $1,000 a year from age twenty until age thirty. (23) Your total

investment would be $10,000. (24) ~~You~~ *If you* received 10 percent interest on your ~~investment.~~ *investment, you* (25) ~~You~~

would now have a total of $15,937. (26) Your interest earnings would be $5,937. (27) You let the

total amount sit in the bank, continuing to earn ~~interest.~~ *interest, and* (28) ~~You~~ don't add another dime to that amount. (29) By age sixty-five, you'd have $447,869. (30) That's a total of $437,869 in interest!

(31) Now you can see why it's never too early to start saving!

Adapted from Cheryl Richardson, *Take Time for Your Life*

Unit 4 Writers' Workshop, page 214

1. Y   Y
   Y   Y
5. She omits the comma when she joins ideas with an *-ing* modifier.

UNIT 5
Choosing the Right Noun, Pronoun, Adjective, Adverb, or Preposition

Chapter 19 Nouns

Part A. Defining Singular and Plural

Practice 1, page 220

The following plural nouns should be listed:

1. notebooks
2. heroes
3. men
4. halves
5. bridges
6. deer
7. runners-up
8. women
9. radios
10. teeth
11. brothers-in-law
12. technicians
13. shelves
14. potatoes
15. mice
16. children
17. flights
18. wives
19. places
20. maids-of-honor

Practice 2, page 220

The following errors should be corrected:

people
(1) Many ~~peoples~~ consider Glacier National Park the jewel of the National Park System.
lakes *wildlife*
(2) Its many mountains, glaciers, waterfalls, blue-green ~~lake~~, and amazing ~~wildlifes~~ are in the
roads
remote Rocky Mountains in the northwest corner of Montana. (3) Several ~~road~~ take visitors into

the park, especially Going-to-the-Sun Road, which clings to the mountainside and offers
feet
spectacular, stomach-churning views. (4) At Logan Pass—6,646 ~~foot~~ high—the road crosses the
Rockies *rivers*
Continental Divide. (5) From this line along the spine of the ~~Rocky~~, all ~~river~~ flow either west to

the Pacific Ocean, south to the Gulf, or east. (6) Because Glacier is truly a wilderness park, it is

women children

best seen by hikers, not drivers. (7) Most men, ~~woman~~, and ~~childs~~ who hike the park's 700 miles of

feet

trails come prepared—with hats, long-sleeved shirts, and on their ~~feets~~, proper hiking shoes.

equipment

(8) Their ~~equipments~~ includes bottled water and, just in case, bear spray. (9) Glacier has a large

population of grizzly bears, which weigh up to 1,400 pounds, have four-inch claws, and dislike

wolves bears

surprises. (10) Besides grizzlies, one might glimpse mountain lions, ~~wolfs~~, black ~~bear~~, white

sheep trout

mountain goats, moose, bighorn ~~sheeps~~, elk, and many smaller mammals. (11) Salmon, ~~trouts~~, and

fish Scientists

other ~~fishs~~ swim the ice-cold rivers and lakes. (12) ~~Scientist~~ worry that the glaciers are melting

too quickly, but Glacier Park remains a treasure.

Part B. Signal Words: Singular and Plural

Practice 3, page 221

The following nouns are possible answers:

1.	map	7.	moment
2.	suitcases	8.	tent
3.	words	9.	governor
4.	pens	10.	family
5.	carton	11.	situations
6.	ticket holders	12.	countries

Practice 4, page 222

The following errors should be corrected:

The Best Medicine

researchers

(1) Many ~~researcher~~ believe that laughter is good for people's health. (2) In fact, some

doctors

~~doctor~~ have concluded that laughter actually helps patients heal faster. (3) To put this theory

hospitals

into practice, several ~~hospital~~ have introduced humor routines into their treatment programs.

program

(4) One ~~programs~~ is a children's clown care unit that operates in seven New York City hospitals.

clowns week

(5) Thirty-five ~~clown~~ from the Big Apple Circus go to the hospitals three times every ~~weeks~~.

children

(6) Few ~~child~~ can keep from laughing at the "rubber chicken soup" and "red nose transplant"

observers

routines. (7) Although the program hasn't been studied scientifically, many ~~observer~~ have

specialists
witnessed its positive effects. (8) However, some ~~specialist~~ are conducting strictly scientific

research on health and laughter. (9) One study, carried out at Loma Linda University in

test
California, has shown the positive effects of laughter on the immune system. (10) Another ~~tests~~,

done at the College of William and Mary in Virginia, has confirmed the California findings.

systems
(11) Other studies in progress are suggesting that all physiological ~~system~~ may be affected

claim
positively by laughter. (12) Finally, research also is backing up a ~~claims~~ made by Norman

Cousins, author of the book *Anatomy of an Illness*. (13) While he was fighting a life-threatening

disease   *studies*
~~diseases~~, Cousins maintained that hearty laughter took away his pain. (14) Several recent ~~study~~

have shown that pain does become less intense when the sufferer responds to comedy.

Part C. Signal Words with OF

Practice 6, page 223

The following nouns are possible answers:

1. students
2. sandals
3. suggestions

4. protesters
5. parents
6. whales

Practice 8, page 224

The following errors should be corrected:

The Fender Sound

(1) If you are a fan of popular music or blues, the guitar sound you have been listening to was

created by Leo Fender. (2) Leo Fender invented the modern amplified guitar, the instrument of

stars
choice for many of today's pop ~~star~~. (3) The instrument that Fender introduced in the 1940s had an

incredible sound—clear, crisp, and clean. (4) Buddy Holly, the Beatles, Jimi Hendrix, and B.B.

performers
King were just a few of the ~~performer~~ who bought and loved a Fender guitar.

(5) Unfortunately, by the time Fender sold his invention to CBS, the famous Fender guitars

had declined in quality and were selling very poorly. (6) William Schultz, who worked for CBS

musicians

at the time, felt that he could turn things around; however, few of the ~~musician~~ who had played

the original Fenders believed he could succeed. (7) He did.

(8) The Telecaster and the Stratocaster have become two of the most famous instruments in

instruments

music history. (9) Approximately 335,000 are sold a year; each of these ~~instrument~~ is considered a

classic. (10) The next time you attend a concert, listen for the Fender sound.

Chapter Review, page 225

The following errors should be corrected:

The Effects of Alcohol on Pregnancy

mothers-to-be *child*

(1) All ~~mother-to-bes~~ who drink alcohol run the risk of harming an innocent ~~children~~.

woman

(2) When a pregnant ~~women~~ takes a drink, the alcohol goes straight from her bloodstream into

drinks

the bloodstream of her child. (3) When she has several ~~drink~~, the blood-alcohol level of her

child rises as high as her own.

ways *infants*

(4) Newborns can be harmed by alcohol in many ~~way~~. (5) Some ~~infant~~ are born addicted to

alcohol and will become alcoholics as adults. (6) Other children are born mentally retarded. (7) In

doctors *causes*

fact, most ~~doctor~~ believe that exposure to alcohol before birth is one of the major ~~cause~~ of mental

retardation. (8) In the worst cases, babies are born with a disease called fetal alcohol syndrome.

(9) These unfortunate children not only are mentally retarded but also can have many physical

deformities

~~deformity~~ as well. (10) In milder cases, the children's problems don't show up until they go to

school. (11) For instance, they may have poor memories and short attention spans. (12) Later, they

job

may have trouble holding a ~~jobs~~.

lives

(13) Too many young ~~life~~ have been ruined before birth because of alcohol consumption.

children *future*

(14) All unborn ~~child~~ need and deserve a chance to have a healthy, normal ~~futures~~. (15) If you are

woman

a ~~women~~ who is expecting a baby, stop drinking alcohol now!

Chapter 20 Pronouns

Part A. Defining Pronouns and Antecedents

Practice 1, page 228

The following pronouns and antecedents should be listed:

Pronoun	Antecedent
1. her	Susan B. Anthony
2. her	Anthony
3. his	President Lincoln
4. they	women
5. she	Anthony
6. it	fine
7. her	Anthony
8. it	Supreme Court
9. their	audiences
10. they	women

Practice 2, page 228

The following antecedents should be listed:

1. journalist
2. Biro
3. pen
4. Biro and his brother

6. pilots
8. department store
10. ballpoints

Part B. Referring to Indefinite Pronouns

Practice 3, page 230

The following pronouns and antecedents should be listed:

1. his or her; citizen
2. he or she; person
3. her; player
4. he or she; anyone
5. their; Fred and Nina

6. his or her; someone
7. their; managers
8. his or her; everyone
9. his or her; nobody
10. his or her; everybody

Practice 4, page 230

The following errors should be corrected:

       his or her
1. Somebody left ~~their~~ bag of popcorn on the seat.

2. C

       his or her
3. Everybody can take ~~their~~ choice of two dishes from column A and one from column B.

his or her
4. No one works harder at ~~their~~ paramedic job than my brother-in-law.

its
5. Each state has ~~their~~ own flag.

6. C

Part C. Referring to Collective Nouns

Practice 6, page 231

The following pronouns and antecedents should be listed:

1. its; company
2. their; teams
3. its; class
4. its; city
5. their; soap operas
6. its; band
7. its; panel
8. its; college

Practice 7, page 232

The following errors should be corrected:

its
1. The computer company retrains ~~their~~ employees for new jobs.

its
2. Central Technical College wants to double ~~their~~ enrollment by 2008.

its
3. That rock group has changed ~~their~~ name for the third time.

4. C

its
5. The gas company plans to move ~~their~~ headquarters again.

6. C

Part D. Referring to Special Singular Constructions

Practice 9, page 233

The following pronouns and antecedents should be listed:

1. his or her; one
2. her; every one
3. its; each
4. his or her; either
5. his; one
6. his or her; neither
7. he or she; every one
8. their; Lin Li and her mother

Practice 10, page 234

The following errors should be corrected:

her
1. One of the women at the hardware counter hasn't made ~~their~~ purchase yet.

         its
2. Each of the birds has ~~their~~ distinctive mating ritual.

3. C

                his
4. I hope that neither of the men will change ~~their~~ vote.

5. C

         her
6. Neither of the women bought ~~their~~ toe ring at Toes R Us.

7. C

        his or her
8. Each of my grandchildren has ~~their~~ own bedroom.

Part E. Avoiding Vague and Repetitious Pronouns

Practice 12, page 235

The following sentences are possible answers:

1. Many dyslexic persons have achieved success in their chosen professions.
2. For example, Albert Einstein was dyslexic.
3. His biography says that he couldn't interpret written words the way others could.
4. His elementary school teachers claimed that he was a slow learner.
5. However, this slow learner changed the way science looked at time and space.
6. C
7. American history teaches us that President Woodrow Wilson and Vice President Nelson Rockefeller were both dyslexic.
8. Authors can have this problem too; the well-known mystery writer Agatha Christie had trouble reading.
9. Finally, several magazines report that both Tom Cruise and Cher are dyslexic.
10. Cher wasn't able to read until she was eighteen years old.

Part F. Using Pronouns as Subjects, Objects, and Possessives

Practice 13, page 238

The following pronouns should be underlined and cases labeled:

  P   *S*   *P*
1. <u>My</u> brother Shadow Hawk and <u>I</u> represent <u>our</u> Kiowa tribe at many powwows, competing in

   the men's traditional dance category.

  S   *O*
2. <u>We</u> wear costume pieces handed down to <u>us</u> from previous generations.

3. Each dancer wears a warrior's feather headdress, called a *roach*, and an impressive bustle of

            P
   feathers tied to <u>his</u> back.

                                                                                          p
4. Because the bustles are made of sacred eagle feathers, spectators stand and remove <u>their</u>
        p
    hats to show <u>their</u> reverence.
                              p   *p*
5. The steady drumbeat provides <u>its</u> rhythm for <u>our</u> movements.
                                                        S   *S*
6. This dance evolved from old forms of war dances, so <u>we</u> use <u>it</u> now to act out the story of a

    battle or a hunt.
                              p   *S*   *p*   *p*
7. Shadow Hawk interprets <u>his</u> story one way, and <u>I</u> interpret <u>mine</u> differently, so <u>our</u>

    movements are individually creative.
        S
8. But <u>we</u> both begin by crouching low to the ground, looking for the tracks of the animal or the

    enemy.
                                  S   *S*
9. The tempo of the drum increases, and <u>he</u> and <u>I</u> speed up our footwork to dramatize stalking
    p
    <u>our</u> prey.
                                                        O   *S*   *p*
10. Acting out the dramatic final challenge means a lot to <u>me</u> because <u>I</u> can express with <u>my</u>
                                                                        S
    movements the bravery, dignity, and pride that <u>I</u> feel.

Part G. Choosing the Correct Case after AND or OR

Practice 14, page 240

The following pronouns should be circled:

1. I
2. me
3. us
4. her
5. me

6. her
7. him
8. me
9. he; me
10. he; she

Practice 15, page 240

The following errors should be corrected:

                I
1. Annie and ~~me~~ enjoy going to the gym every day.
    She   *I*
2. ~~Her~~ and ~~me~~ have tried every class, from kickboxing to spinning.
                        me
3. Between you and ~~I~~, I favor hydrobox, which is kickboxing in water.
    We
4. ~~Us~~ and our friends also use the pool for water aerobics.

5. C

                                                                me

6. Stationary cycling sometimes feels boring to Annie and ~~I~~.

                                              her   *me*

7. On the other hand, it is a good time for ~~she~~ and ~~I~~ to daydream.

8. C

                                   he

9. I am not sure whether ~~him~~ or weightlifting makes her sweat so much.

10. C

Part H. Choosing the Correct Case in Comparisons

Practice 16, page 241

The following pronouns should be circled:

1. I	6. them
2. him	7. she
3. I	8. they
4. he	9. we
5. he	10. him

Practice 17, page 242

The following errors should be corrected:

                                                 we

1. Ben walked to Death Valley more slowly than ~~us~~.

                                              I

2. Jean can sing Haitian folk songs better than ~~me~~.

3. C

                                               she

4. Sarah was surprised that Joyce paid more than ~~her~~ for a ticket.

5. C

                                                                             he

6. Before switching jobs, I wanted to know if Rose would be as good a supervisor as ~~him~~.

                                            me

7. The night shift suits her better than ~~I~~.

                                                            she

8. Antoinette is six feet tall; no one on the loading dock is taller than ~~her~~.

Part I. Using Pronouns with -SELF and -SELVES

Practice 19, page 243

The following pronouns should be listed:

1. ourselves
2. himself
3. yourselves
4. yourself
5. themselves

6. herself
7. herself
8. themselves
9. itself
10. himself

Chapter Review, page 245

The following errors should be corrected:

A New Beginning

(1) Martha Andrews/~~she~~ was a good student in high school. (2) After graduation, she found a

job as a bank teller in order to save money for college. (3) She liked her job because she knew her

their
regular customers and enjoyed handling ~~his or her~~ business. (4) When she was nineteen, Patrick

she
Kelvin, another teller, and ~~her~~ fell in love and married. (5) By the time she was twenty-two, she

had become the mother of three children. (6) Martha's plans for college faded.

(7) As her fortieth birthday approached, Martha began thinking about going to college in

order to study accounting; however, she had many fears. (8) Would she remember how to study

she
after so many years? (9) Would the younger students be smarter than ~~her~~? (10) Would she feel out

of place with them? (11) Worst of all, her husband/~~he~~ worried that Martha would neglect him.

his or her
(12) He thought that everyone who goes to college forgot ~~their~~ family. (13) He also feared that

he
Martha would be more successful than ~~him~~.

himself
(14) One of Martha's children, who attended college ~~hisself~~, encouraged her. (15) With

an adviser
his help, Martha got the courage to visit Middleton College. (16) In the admissions office, ~~they~~

told her that older students were valued at Middleton. (17) Older students often enriched classes

they
because ~~he or she~~ brought a wealth of life experiences with them. (18) Martha also learned that

its
the college had a special program to help ~~their~~ older students adjust to school.

she
(19) Martha enrolled in college the next fall. (20) To their credit, ~~her~~ and her husband soon

realized that they had made the right decision.

Chapter 21 Adjectives and Adverbs

Part A. Defining and Writing Adjectives and Adverbs

Practice 1, page 248

The following adjectives are possible choices:

1. energetic
2. orange
3. Sarcastic
4. old
5. bitter

Practice 2, page 248

The following adverbs are possible choices:

1. quickly
2. constantly
3. convincingly
4. madly
5. Quietly

Practice 3, page 249

The following adverbs should be listed:

1. honestly
2. loudly
3. easily
4. carefully
5. creatively
6. quickly
7. perfectly
8. really
9. eagerly
10. joyfully

Practice 4, page 249

The following adjectives and adverbs should be circled:

1. remote
2. actually
3. abundant
4. completely
5. rare
6. slowly
7. lazily
8. amazing
9. comically
10. gracefully
11. easily
12. famous
13. perfect
14. spectacular, fabulous
15. gently

Part B. A Troublesome Pair: GOOD/WELL

Practice 6, page 251

The following adjectives and adverbs should be listed:

1. good
2. well
3. well
4. well
5. good
6. well

7. well
8. good
9. good
10. well
11. good
12. good, well

Part C. Writing Comparatives

Practice 7, page 252

The following comparative forms should be listed:

1. faster
2. more interesting
3. more hopeful
4. sweeter

5. thicker
6. more modern
7. more valuable
8. colder

Practice 8, page 252

The following comparative forms should be listed:

1. shinier
2. friendlier
3. lazier
4. easier

5. fancier
6. luckier
7. livelier
8. crazier

Practice 9, page 253

1. Her new boss is fussier than her previous one.
2. The trail was rockier than we expected.
3. The people in my new neighborhood are friendlier than those in my old one.
4. Magda has a more cheerful personality than her sister.
5. I have never seen a duller TV program than this one.
6. The audience at this theater is noisier than usual.
7. His jacket is newer than Rudy's.
8. If today is warmer than yesterday, we'll picnic on the lawn.

Part D. Writing Superlatives

Practice 11, page 254

The following superlatives should be listed:

1. loudest
2. most colorful
3. bravest
4. strongest
5. most brilliant

6. wildest
7. most practical
8. most frightening
9. greenest
10. haziest

Practice 12, page 254

1. My nephew is the most thoughtful teenager I know.
2. Mercury is the closest planet to the sun.
3. This baby makes the oddest gurgling noises we have ever heard.
4. Jackie always makes us laugh, but she is funniest when she hasn't had enough sleep.
5. When I finally started college, I was the most eager student on campus.
6. Ms. Dross raises the strangest reptiles in her basement.
7. This peach is the ripest in the basket.
8. He thinks that the most successful people are just lucky.

Part E. Troublesome Comparatives and Superlatives

Practice 13, page 255

The following comparatives and superlatives should be listed:

1. better
2. best
3. worse
4. worst
5. worse

6. better
7. worse
8. worst
9. better
10. better, worse

Part F. Demonstrative Adjectives: THIS/THAT and THESE/THOSE

Practice 14, page 256

The following demonstrative adjectives should be circled:

1. These
2. this
3. those
4. that

5. those
6. this, that
7. that
8. This

Chapter Review, page 257

The following errors should be corrected:

A. (1) The most ~~famousest~~ *famous* comet, Halley's comet, appears ~~regular~~ *regularly* every seventy-six years.

(2) This mass of gas and dust has caused panic and fear because its appearance has often coincided with the ~~baddest~~ *worst* events in history. (3) During the Middle Ages, people believed that Halley's comet was a ~~surely~~ *sure* omen of destruction. (4) The ~~most silly~~ *silliest* notions about Halley's comet came about during its 1910 appearance when people bought pills and bottled oxygen to protect themselves. (5) Although that sounds ~~real~~ *really* foolish, they believed that poisonous gas was contained in the comet's ~~brilliantly~~ *brilliant* tail. (6) Despite the ~~most wildest~~ *wildest* superstitions, Halley's comet has given us ~~more better~~ *better* information about comets and our solar system.

B. (1) One of the ~~real~~ *really* inspirational stories of recent years is the story of Lance Armstrong.

(2) In 1993, Armstrong became the World Cycling champion. (3) In 1999, he won the 2,287-mile Tour de France, the world's ~~most greatest~~ *greatest* bike race. (4) Between those two events, however, he won something that was even more ~~importanter~~ *important*.

(5) In 1996, Lance Armstrong was diagnosed with testicular cancer. (6) The cancer spread to his brain, abdomen, and lungs. (7) He was given only a 40 percent chance of surviving and even ~~worser~~ *worse* odds of ever returning to biking. (8) According to his doctors, however, he approached his cancer with the same skills he used for competitive sports: discipline, persistence, sacrifice. (9) Armstrong ~~courageous~~ *courageously* went through brain surgery and incredibly painful chemotherapy, but he also continued training. (10) Two years later, he became only the second American to win the twenty-one day Tour de France. (11) ~~More stronger~~ *Stronger* than ever, Armstrong finished seven minutes and thirty-seven seconds ahead of his ~~most nearest~~ *nearest* competitor. (12) Astonishingly enough, he went on to win the Tour de France the following year and an Olympic bronze in 2000. (13) Although some people believe that cancer is the ~~worsest~~ *worst* thing that can happen, Armstrong maintains that cancer is the ~~most best~~ *best* thing that ever happened to him. (14) In his

book, *It's Not about the Bike*, he writes that without ~~those~~ *that* disease he would not have married or

had a child. (15) When you face death, he says, your focus becomes really clear.

Chapter 22 Prepositions

Part A. Defining and Working with Prepositional Phrases

Practice 1, page 260

The following prepositional phrases should be underlined:

1. about human biology
2. at midday
3. In extreme cold,
4. of body weight
5. of us
6. in summer
7. of every ten people
8. of blood
9. on the human body
10. with an extra rib

Part B. Troublesome Prepositions: IN, ON, and LIKE

Practice 2, page 261

1. on, to
2. to, for
3. by, through, across, over
4. In, like, with
5. into, up, to
6. by, of, toward
7. After, in , on, in
8. from, to, until
9. in, on
10. above, with, around

Part C. Prepositions in Common Expressions

Practice 3, page 264

The following expressions should be circled:

1. consisted of
2. approve of
3. applied for
4. displeased with
5. depend on
6. succeed in
7. interested in
8. grateful to
9. fond of
10. dealt with
11. took advantage of
12. responsible for

Chapter Review, page 265

The following corrections should be made:

Listening for Life Among the Stars

(1) ~~On~~ *In* the film *Contact,* actress Jodie Foster plays a scientist searching for intelligent life ~~at~~ *in* the universe. (2) Foster's character is not real. (3) However, she is very similar ~~of~~ *to* Dr. Jill Tarter, research director at SETI, the Search for Extraterrestrial Intelligence Institute. (4) Dr. Tarter and her team listen for radio signals sent ~~off~~ *from* outer space because such signals might prove that life exists among the stars.

(5) Dr. Tarter earned her degrees ~~across~~ *in* engineering and physics ~~upon~~ *in* the 1960s and 1970s. (6) After completing her education, she worked for the space agency. (7) Then she heard ~~off~~ *of* a new program specializing ~~on~~ *in* the search for life ~~at~~ *in* space. (8) Dr. Tarter was greatly interested ~~of~~ *in* this exciting program. (9) Since then, she has spent more hours gazing ~~onto~~ *into* a telescope than anyone else ~~under~~ *on* the planet.

(10) To scan even bigger areas of space, Dr. Tarter led the development of the Allen Telescope Array ~~on~~ *in* California. (11) This group of telescopes searches twenty-four hours a day for communications from deep space. (12) Dr. Tarter is also raising funds ~~for~~ *to* build a radio telescope ten times more powerful than any used today. (13) She hopes that soon astronauts will install a radio telescope ~~in~~ *on* the moon. (14) Dr. Tarter maintains a sense of humor ~~around~~ *about* her unusual career. (15) When people tease her ~~of~~ *about* her search for "little green men," she laughingly replies ~~at~~ *to* these skeptics that she might find "big blue women" instead.

Unit 5 Review

Proofreading, page 268

The following corrections should be made:

The Last Frontier

(1) When the government of Brazil opened the Amazon rain forest for settlement ~~on~~ *in* the 1970s, ~~they~~ *it* created the last frontier on earth. (2) Many concerned ~~man~~ *men* and ~~woman~~ *women* everywhere now fear that the move has been a ~~disasters~~ *disaster* for the land and for the people. (3) The ~~most large~~ *largest* rain forest in the world, the Amazon rain forest has been hit ~~real~~ *really* hard. (4) The government built highways to make it ~~more easy~~ *easier* for poor people to get to the land, but the roads also made investors interested ~~to~~ *in* the forest. (5) Lumber companies chopped down millions of ~~tree.~~ *trees.* (6) Ranchers and the settlers ~~theirselves~~ *themselves* burned the forest to make room for cattle and crops. (7) All ~~this~~ *these* activities have taken their toll: in one area, which is the size of Colorado, three-quarters of the rain forest has already been destroyed. (8) Many kinds of plants and animals have been lost forever. (9) ~~As~~ *Like* the rain forest itself, the Indians who live ~~they~~ *there* are threatened by this wholesale destruction. (10) Ranchers, miners, loggers, and settlers have moved onto Indian lands.

(11) Contact with the outside world has changed the Indians' traditional way of life. (12) A few Indian ~~tribe~~ *tribes* have made economic and political gains; however, many tribes have totally disappeared.

(13) Many of the ~~settler~~ *settlers* are not doing very ~~good~~ *well* either. (14) People have poured into the region too ~~rapid~~ *rapidly*, and the government is unable to provide the needed services. (15) Small villages have become crowded cities, diseases (especially malaria) have spread, and lawlessness is common. (16) ~~Worse~~ *Worst* of all, the soil beneath the rain forest is not fertile. (17) After a few years, the settlers' ~~land, it~~ *land* is worthless. (18) As the settlers go into debt, businesses take advantage ~~for~~ *of* the situation by buying land ~~quick~~ *quickly* and exploiting it ~~bad~~ *badly*.

(19) Can the situation in the rain forest improve? (20) Although the Brazilian government

that

has been trying to preserve ~~those~~ forest, thousands of fires are still set every year to clear land for

cattle grazing, planting, and building. (21) On the more hopeful side, however, scientists have

extremely

discovered fruits in the rain forest that are ~~extreme~~ high in vitamins and proteins. (22) Those

fruits would be much better crops for the rain forest than the corn, rice, and beans that farmers are

nervously   *most precious*

growing now. (23) The world watches ~~nervous~~. (24) Will the Earth's ~~preciousest~~ rain forest

survive?

Transforming, page 269

The following changes should be made:

Saint Bernards are   *dogs*   *their*

(1) ~~The Saint Bernard is~~ a legendary ~~dog~~ famous for ~~its~~ many acts of bravery. (2) Bred in the

they

wild mountains of Switzerland, ~~it~~ can find paths in the worst snowstorms, smell human beings

These   *creatures*

buried in snow, and detect avalanches before they occur. (3) ~~This~~ powerful yet sensitive ~~creature~~

work   *Saint Bernards find*   *they lie*

~~works~~ in rescue patrols. (4) When ~~a Saint Bernard finds~~ a hurt traveler, ~~it lies~~ down next to the

lick   *Other*

sufferer to keep him or her warm and ~~licks~~ the person's face to restore consciousness. (5) ~~Another~~

dogs go

~~dog goes~~ back to headquarters to sound the alarm and guide a rescue party to the scene. (6) In all,

Saint Bernards have   *these dogs*

~~the Saint Bernard has~~ saved more than two thousand lives. (7) Oddly enough, though ~~this dog~~

have   *Saint Bernards*   *their*

~~has~~ been known for about three hundred years, ~~the Saint Bernard~~ did not get ~~its~~ name until about a

Saint Bernards were

hundred years ago. (8) ~~The Saint Bernard was~~ named for a shelter in the Swiss Alps. (9) Monks of

these dogs

the shelter of Saint Bernard used ~~this dog~~ in rescue patrols.

Unit 5 Writers' Workshop, page 270

1. Y   N
   Y   Y
3. Aim for less repetition and more fresh facts and details.
5. No grammar errors.

UNIT 6
Revising for Consistency and Parallelism

Chapter 23 Consistent Tense

Practice 1, page 275

The following verbs should be underlined and tense inconsistencies corrected:

1. We <u>were walking</u> near the lake when a large moose <u>appears</u> just ahead.
   appeared

2. When Bill <u>asks</u> the time, the cab driver <u>told</u> us it <u>was</u> after six.
   asked

3. The woman on the red bicycle <u>was delivering</u> newspapers while she <u>is enjoying</u> the morning sunshine.
   was

4. Dr. Choi smiled and <u>welcomes</u> the next patient.
   welcomed

5. The Oklahoma prairie <u>stretches</u> for miles, flat and rusty red. Here and there, an oil rig <u>broke</u> the monotony.
   breaks

6. They <u>were strolling</u> down Main Street when the lights <u>go</u> out.
   went

7. My cousins <u>questioned</u> me for hours about my trip. I <u>describe</u> the flight, my impressions of Paris, and every meal I <u>ate</u>.
   described

8. We <u>started cheering</u> as he <u>approaches</u> the finish line.
   approached

9. If Terry <u>takes</u> short naps during the day, she <u>didn't</u> feel tired in the evening.
   doesn't

10. Yesterday, we <u>find</u> the book we <u>need</u> online. We <u>ordered</u> it immediately.
    found   *needed*

Chapter Review, page 276

The following inconsistent verb tenses should be corrected:

A. (1) Self-confidence is vital to success both in childhood and in adulthood. (2) With self-
know
confidence, children ~~knew~~ that they are worthwhile and that they have important goals.
need
(3) Parents can teach their children self-confidence in several ways. (4) First, children ~~needed~~
draw,
praise. (5) When they ~~drew,~~ for example, parents can tell them how beautiful their drawings are.
have
(6) The praise lets them know they ~~had~~ talents that other people admire. (7) Second, children
require   *find*
~~required~~ exposure to many different experiences. (8) They soon ~~found~~ that they need not be afraid
realize
to try new things. (9) They ~~realized~~ that they can succeed as well at chess as they do at
discover
basketball. (10) They ~~discovered~~ that a trip to a museum to examine medieval armor is
                                                                          is
fascinating or that they enjoy taking a class in pottery. (11) Finally, it ~~was~~ very important to
                                                          do
treat children individually. (12) Sensitive parents ~~did~~ not compare their children's successes or

failures with those of their brothers or sisters, relatives, or friends. (13) Of course, parents should

inform children if their behavior or performance in school needs improvement. (14) Parents
help
~~helped~~ children do better, however, by showing them how much they have accomplished so far

and by suggesting how much they can and will accomplish in the future.

B. (1) Last summer, we visited one of the world's oddest museums, the home of someone who

never existed. (2) Early one afternoon, we walked along the real Baker Street in London, England.
loomed
(3) Suddenly, it ~~looms~~ in front of us: number 221B, Mrs. Hudson's boarding house, home of the

famous but fictitious detective Sherlock Holmes. (4) Once inside the perfect reproduction of
were
Holmes' rooms, we ~~are~~ astonished to find all of Holmes' belongings, including his violin, his
learned
walking stick, and his chemistry set. (5) We ~~learn~~ that the founders of the museum had searched
succeeded
the country for Victorian objects and furniture like those in the Holmes stories. (6) They ~~succeed~~
located
beyond any Sherlock Holmes fan's wildest dreams. (7) They ~~locate~~ a Persian slipper like the one
uncovered
in which Holmes stored pipe tobacco. (8) They even ~~uncover~~ a gold and emerald tie pin like the

one Queen Victoria gave Holmes. (9) The museum also had quarters for Holmes' friend and *bought*

assistant, Dr. Watson. (10) For him, the founders ~~buy~~ nineteenth-century medical supplies and

returned

surgical instruments. (11) After we ~~return~~ home that summer, I reread several Sherlock Holmes

saw

stories. (12) In my mind's eye, I ~~see~~ Holmes' rooms and belongings more vividly than ever before.

(13) Of course, Holmes would have predicted that. (14) "Elementary," he would have said.

C. (1) Almost every major city in the world has a subway system. (2) Underground trains

carry

speed through complex networks of tunnels and ~~carried~~ millions of passengers every day.

(3) Subway systems sometimes differ because of their locations. (4) In Mexico City, for

travel

example, subway cars ~~traveled~~ through suspended tunnels capable of absorbing earthquake

runs

shocks. (5) Residents of Haifa, Israel, use an unusually short, straight subway that ~~run~~ up and

brings

down inside a mountain. (6) The train ~~brought~~ people from Haifa's lower port city up—a thousand

feet—to the upper residential city. (7) In Hong Kong, the world's first completely air-conditioned

offers

subway system ~~offered~~ relief from extremely hot and humid outdoor temperatures. (8) Cities like

San Francisco, of course, expand the definition of subway to cover underwater as well as

underground transportation. (9) The San Francisco Bay Area Rapid Transit system (BART)

includes

~~included~~ several miles of track under San Francisco Bay.

(10) Some subway systems are famous for their artwork. (11) With paintings and walls of

look

precious marble, many Moscow subway stations ~~looked~~ like museums. (12) Several stations in

seem

Stockholm, Sweden, ~~seemed~~ like elegant caverns because of granite carvings and rock in its natural

state. (13) With colorful designs and all kinds of special effects, subway stations from Montreal to

resemble

Tokyo ~~resembled~~ modern art galleries.

do

(14) Subways, therefore, ~~did~~ more than provide an efficient means of public transportation.

(15) They are creative solutions to special problems as well as expressions of art and culture.

Chapter 24 Consistent Person

Practice 1, page 279

The following inconsistencies of person and verb tense should be corrected:

1. Belkys treats me like family when I visit her. She always makes ~~you~~ *me* feel at home.

2. I love to go dancing. ~~You~~ *I* can exercise, work off tensions, and have fun, all at the same time.

3. If a person has gone to a large high school, ~~you~~ *he or she* may find a small college a welcome change.

4. When Lee and I drive to work at 6 a.m., ~~you~~ *we* see the city waking up.

5. Every mechanic should make sure ~~they have~~ *he or she has* a good set of tools.

6. People who want to buy cars today are often stopped by high prices. ~~You~~ *They* aren't sure how to get the most for ~~your~~ *their* money.

7. Do each of you have ~~his or her~~ *your* own e-mail address?

8. Many people think that ~~your~~ *their* vote doesn't really count.

9. A teacher's attitude affects the performance of ~~their~~ *his or her* students.

10. It took me three years to decide to enroll in college; in many ways, ~~you~~ *I* really didn't know what ~~you~~ *I* wanted to do when ~~you~~ *I* finished high school.

Chapter Review, page 281

The following inconsistencies of person and verb tense should be corrected:

A. (1) When exam time comes, do you become anxious because you aren't sure how to study for tests? (2) ~~They~~ *You* may have done all the work for ~~their~~ *your* courses, but you still don't feel prepared. (3) Fortunately, ~~he~~ *you* can do some things to make taking tests easier. (4) ~~They~~ *You* can look through the textbook and review the material ~~one has~~ *you have* underlined. (5) You might read the notes you have taken in class and highlight or underline main points. (6) ~~A person~~ *You* can think about some questions the professor may ask and then try writing answers. (7) Sometimes, ~~they~~ *you* can find other people from your class and form a study group to compare class notes. (8) The night before a test, ~~they~~ *you*

You
shouldn't drink too much coffee. (9) ~~They~~ should get a good night's sleep so that your mind will be

as sharp for the exam as your pencil.

B. (1) The sport of mountain biking began in northern California in the 1970s. (2) Some
their
experienced cyclists began using ~~his or her~~ old one-speed fat-tire bikes to explore dirt roads and
They
trails. (3) ~~You~~ began by getting car rides up one of the mountains and pedaling their bikes down.
they
(4) Then they began cycling farther up the mountain until ~~he and she~~ were pedaling to the top.
their
(5) Those cyclists eventually started designing bikes to fit ~~our~~ sport. (6) By the end of the 1970s,
they
road bike manufacturers decided ~~you~~ would join the action. (7) By the mid-1980s, mountain biking

had become a national craze, and sales of mountain bikes were exceeding sales of road bikes.
they
(8) Today, mountain bikers pay about $1,000 for bikes that have everything ~~we~~ need for

riding on rough trails: front-wheel shock absorbers, twenty-four gears that shift easily, a
their
lightweight frame, flexible wheels, and even a full suspension frame. (9) Cyclists ride ~~your~~ bikes

everywhere; some of their favorite places are South Dakota's Badlands, Colorado's ski resorts,
They
and Utah's Canyonlands National Park. (10) ~~You~~ compete in mountain bike races all over the
them
world. (11) To top this off, in 1996 some of ~~you~~ competed in the first Olympic mountain bike race,

outside Atlanta, Georgia. (12) The course, which had tightly spaced trees and large rocks,

included steep climbs and sharp descents with surprise jumps. (13) What were those early
they
"inventors" thinking as ~~he and she~~ watched that first Olympic race?

Chapter 25 Parallelism

Part A. Writing Parallel Constructions

Practice 1, page 284

The following nonparallel elements should be circled:

1. runner
2. my four dogs
3. painting the kitchen
4. work

5. toward the audience
6. buying a birthday present
7. dressed for the office
8. We are baking a cake tonight.

Practice 2, page 285

1. Many people believe that they will be happy once they have money, fame, a spouse, or a good job.
2. Psychologist Martin Seligman found that gratitude is a key ingredient of happiness and invented the "gratitude visit."
3. First, you think of a person who was truly helpful to you, and then you write a "gratitude letter" to that person.
4. In this letter, explain sincerely and specifically why you are grateful.
5. Then visit this person and read your letter aloud.
6. According to Seligman, the ritual is moving, powerful, and emotional.
7. Seligman says people feel happier if they focus on the positive aspects of the past rather than on the negative.
8. Gratitude visits, he believes, increase the intensity, the length, and the frequency of positive memories.
9. In addition, they tend to inspire the receivers of thanks to become givers of thanks.
10. One gratitude visit leads to another, creating a chain of appreciation and contentment for everyone.

Practice 3, page 286

The following answers are possible choices:

1. yellow; green
2. sat by the window; played cards
3. she was always right; everyone else was always wrong
4. love to hike; love to sing
5. spend most of their time together; pursue separate interests
6. flies a plane; fly my kite
7. through the day; into the night
8. Playing the piano; lying on the beach
9. delicate shells; smooth stones; broken glass
10. paint the walls; wallpaper the room

Chapter Review, page 287

The following errors in parallel structure should be corrected:

Chinese Medicine in the United States

(1) When diplomatic relations between the United States and mainland China were restored
in 1972, acupuncture was one import that sparked America's imagination and ~~made people~~ *interest.* ~~interested.~~ (2) In the United States today, the most popular form of Chinese medicine is acupuncture.

(3) Acupuncture involves the insertion of thin, sterile, ~~made of~~ stainless steel needles at specific points on the body. (4) Chinese medical science believes that the *chi,* or life force, can be

manipulating

redicted by inserting and ~~by the manipulation of~~ these needles. (5) They are inserted to just

left

below the skin and are either removed quickly or ~~leave them~~ in for up to forty minutes. (6) In

charge

addition, the acupuncturist can twirl them, heat them, or ~~charging~~ them with a mild electrical

current. (7) Acupuncture can reduce pain for those suffering from allergies, arthritis, backache, or

~~with a~~ toothache. (8) It also has helped in cases of chronic substance abuse, anxiety, and ~~for~~

depression

~~depressed people~~.

importance

(9) Chinese medicine has grown in popularity and ~~become important~~ in America. (10) Thirty-

five schools in the United States teach Chinese acupuncture. (11) Forty-four states have passed

license

laws that regulate or ~~for licensing~~ the practice of acupuncture. (12) Since 1974, the government has

reliability

authorized several studies of acupuncture's effectiveness and ~~how reliable it is~~. (13) Although

research has failed to explain how acupuncture works, it has confirmed that it does work.

used.

(14) The studies also suggest that acupuncture should continue to be tested and ~~using it~~.

Unit 6 Review

Proofreading, page 290

The following errors in tense and parallel structure should be corrected:

A.   Inspiration

had

(1) When I was a freshman in high school, I ~~have~~ a serious problem with English.

(2) All day long, my head was filled with ideas for compositions, but when I arrived in

went

English class, my mind ~~goes~~ blank. (3) I feared that my teacher thought I was just another lazy

student. (4) In fact, I almost gave up; thank goodness, I didn't!

found   *went*

(5) Then, by the strangest twist of fate, I ~~find~~ out why my mind ~~goes~~ blank and why my

compositions were never finished. (6) One day, the English class moved from the basement to the

saw the window

third floor of the building. (7) The moment I stepped into the new room and ~~the window was seen~~, I

knew

~~know~~ what had bothered me all semester—no light, no fresh air, and ~~the fact that there wasn't a~~

no   *selected*

~~sense of~~ space. (8) I ~~select~~ a seat near the window and looked over my shoulder at the tall oak tree that stretched past the third-floor window. (9) When I ~~pick~~ *picked* up my pen, the writing began to flow.

(10) If I ran out of things to say, I just ~~glance~~ *glanced* over my shoulder at the tree and at the sky—and I

~~would be~~ *was* inspired to continue my essay.

Christopher Moore, student

B.   Opening Up the Workplace

(1) New technology is helping people with disabilities enter the workforce in record

numbers. (2) With the latest products, blind workers can see a computer screen, and deaf workers

can ~~be hearing~~ *hear* a telephone call. (3) People who cannot speak can talk to others. (4) People operate

a computer even if ~~your~~ *their* fingers cannot type. (5) Pitney Bowes, Toshiba, Apple Computer, and other

companies are creating a workforce revolution with "assistive technology."

(6) For example, if workers cannot move their arms or legs, ~~he or she~~ *they* can use an eye-gaze

program. (7) They can direct a laser beam to points on ~~his or her~~ *their* computer screens just by *looking* at

control keys. (8) The laser sets off commands for the computer to follow. (9) Users need only keep

their heads still and ~~controlling one eye is also necessary~~ *control one eye.*

(10) Some computers display information in Braille for blind people or ~~the print is~~ in

extremely large print for those with vision problems. (11) Some software programs convert written

text into speech so that blind workers can hear it. (12) Other products convert speech into written

text so that deaf workers can see it.

(13) Assistive technology will also benefit the company's aging workforce. (14) Experts

estimate that nearly two-thirds of the population will eventually suffer partial or ~~it may be~~

total hearing loss. (15) Glaucoma and ~~getting~~ cataracts will threaten vision. (16) Stroke victims

may find ~~ourselves~~ *themselves* unable to communicate or ~~functioning~~ *function* independently. (17) The new technology

will bring people into the workforce *and* ~~kept~~ *keep* them there.

Unit 6 Writers' Workshop, page 292

1. Y   Y
       Y   Y
2. She is a fly addressing flies about to enter Peck's apartment.
4. (1) a guide to the rooms; (2) advice about the homeowner
7. No errors.

UNIT 7
Mastering Mechanics

Chapter 26 Capitalization

Practice 1, page 298

The following capitalization errors should be corrected:

          C   *P*   *R*   *H*   *N* *Y*

1. Richard carmona grew up in a poor puerto rican family in harlem, new york.

                                                    D   *C*   *H* *S*

2. He started skipping classes in middle school and dropped out of dewitt clinton high school

   at age seventeen.

3. Carmona worked at dull, low-paying jobs until a conversation with a young man on leave

       U.S. A

   from the u.s. army changed his life.

4. This soldier inspired him to join the military in 1967, and Carmona soon found himself

                   V

   working as a medic in vietnam.

           G   *B*   *P*   *H*

5. He joined the green berets, earning two purple hearts for his brave service.

            A   *B*

6. Carmona returned to america determined to become a doctor, so he enrolled at bronx

   C   *C*

   community college.

7. He says that he owes his career to that college and to several of its professors—including

   M   *S*   *R*   *K*

   michael steuerman and richard kor, who inspired him to succeed.

8. Carmona went on to earn degrees in biology and chemistry; he attended medical school at the

   U   *C*

   university of california, graduating first in his class in three years instead of four.

                                                U   *A*

9. Even after becoming a trauma surgeon and professor at the university of arizona, he continued

   to use his military training and knowledge of special operations.

                                    P   *C*   *S*

10. This crime-fighting doctor joined the S.W.A.T. team for the pima county sheriff's
    D
    department in 1986.

11. Carmona made headlines in 1992 when he dangled out of a helicopter to rescue a person

    stranded on the side of a cliff, an event that inspired a television movie.
                                    T   *A*

12. In 1999, he stopped at a traffic accident in tucson, arizona; saw a hostage taker holding a

    woman at gunpoint; and shot the suspect.
                                      S   *P*   *G*   *W B*

13. Less than a year after the terrorist attacks of september 11, 2001, president george w. bush
          D C
    selected dr. carmona for the country's top medical post, noting his knowledge of law

    enforcement, bioterrorism, and emergency preparedness.
              L   *U.S. S*   *G*

14. The second latino to be named to the post, u.s. surgeon general Carmona thanked the
                     S   *E*
    president in both spanish and english.
        J   *M C*   *U.S. C*   *C*

15. Senator john mccain said in the u.s. congress that carmona is "the embodiment of the
    A
    american dream."

Chapter Review, page 300

The following capitalization errors should be corrected:

The Strange Career of Deborah Sampson

      s
(1) Few Soldiers have had a stranger army career than Deborah Sampson. (2) Sampson
                                                  R   *W*   *D*
disguised herself as a man so that she could fight in the revolutionary war. (3) Born on december
                                         t   *P*   *M*   *f*
17, 1760, she spent her early years in a Town near plymouth, massachusetts. (4) Her Father left

his large family, however, and went to sea when Sampson was seven years old. (5) After living
   c   *m*   *S*
with a Cousin and then with the widow of a Minister, sampson became a servant in a wealthy

family.

    (6) Household tasks and hard outdoor work built up her physical strength. (7) She was
                    m   *w*
taller than the average Man and more muscular than the average Woman. (8) Therefore, she was
                                            C   *A*   *M*
able to disguise herself successfully. (9) Sampson enlisted in the continental army on may 20, 1782,
             R   *S*
under the name of robert shurtleff.

(10) Sampson fought in several Battles and was wounded at least twice. (11) One story says
that she took a bullet out of her own leg with a penknife to avoid seeing a Doctor. (12) However,
after the surrender of the british, Sampson's regiment was sent to philadelphia, where she was
hospitalized with a high fever and lost consciousness. (13) At the Hospital, dr. Barnabas Binney
made the discovery that ended Sampson's army life. (14) She was honorably discharged by
general henry knox at west point on october 28, 1783.

(15) Officially female again, Sampson returned to Massachusetts and eventually married a
Farmer named benjamin gannett. (16) The story of Sampson's adventures spread; in 1797, a book
titled *the female review* was published about her. (17) When Sampson decided to earn money by
telling her own story, she became the first american woman to be paid as a Public Speaker.
(18) She gave her first talk at the federal street theatre in boston in march 1802 and toured until
september. (19) Her health was poor, however, and she could not continue her appearances.
(20) In 1804, paul revere, who was a neighbor of the gannetts, wrote to a member of the united
states congress. (21) He asked for a pension for this Soldier who had never been paid and was still
suffering from her war wounds. (22) Congress granted deborah sampson gannett a pension of four
dollars a month.

(23) Deborah Sampson died in sharon, Massachusetts, in april 1827. (24) Her story inspired
the People of her own time and continues to inspire People today. (25) Two plays have been
written about her: *she was there* and *portrait of deborah*. (26) On veterans day in 1989, a life-size
bronze statue was dedicated in front of the sharon public library to honor her.

Chapter 27 Commas

Part A. Commas after Items in a Series

Practice 1, page 303

The following commas should be added:

1. shoes, socks,
2. Sylvia, Eric,
3. accounts, strategy,
4. Florida, Brazil,

5. porch, basement,
6. photographs, diaries,
7. Spinning, kickboxing,
8. hook, coat,

Part B. Commas after Introductory Phrases

Practice 3, page 304

The following commas should be added:

1. rainstorm,
2. p.m.,
3. trip,
4. C

5. moon,
6. break,
7. pool,
8. time,

Part C. Commas for Direct Address

Practice 5, page 304

The following persons should be circled and commas added:

1. I am happy to inform you, (Mr. Forbes), that you are the father of twins.

2. We expect to return on Monday, (Miguel.)

3. It appears, (my friend), that you have won two tickets to the opera.

4. Get out of my roast, (you mangy old dog.)

5. (Tom), it's probably best that you sell the old car at a loss.

6. If I were you, (Hilda), I would wait to make the phone call until we are off the highway.

7. (Bruce), it's time you learned to operate the lawn mower!

8. I am pleased to announce, (ladies and gentlemen), that Madonna is our surprise guest tonight.

Part D. Commas to Set Off Appositives

Practice 7, page 305

The following appositives should be circled and commas added:

1. That door, (the one with the X on it), leads backstage.

2. (A short man), he decided not to pick a fight with the basketball player.

3. Hassim, (my friend from Morocco), will be staying with me this week.

4. My nephew wants to go to Mama's Indoor Arcade, (a very noisy place.)

5. George Eliot, (a nineteenth-century novelist), was a woman named Mary Ann Evans.

6. (A very close race), the election for mayor wasn't decided until 2 a.m.

7. On the Fourth of July, (my favorite holiday), my high school friends get together for an all-day barbecue.

8. Dr. Simpson, (a specialist in ethnic music), always travels with a tape recorder.

Part E. Commas for Parenthetical Expressions

Practice 9, page 306

The following parenthetical expressions should be circled and commas added:

1. (Believe me), Sonia has studied hard for her driver's test.

2. She possesses, (it would seem), an uncanny gift for gab.

3. It was, (I assure you), an accident.

4. (To tell the truth), I just put a treadmill in your basement.

5. Her supervisor, (by the way), will never admit when he is wrong.

6. A well-prepared résumé, (as a matter of fact), can help you get a job.

7. He is, (in fact), a black belt.

8. (To begin with), you need a new carburetor.

Part F. Commas for Dates

Practice 11, page 307

The following commas should be added:

1. By Tuesday, October 6, he had outlined the whole history text.
2. Thursday, May 8, is Hereford's birthday.
3. She was born on January 9, 1985, in a small New England town.
4. He was born on July 4, 1976, the two-hundredth anniversary of the Declaration of Independence.
5. C
6. On January 24, 1848, James Wilson Marshall found gold in California.
7. C
8. Charles Schulz's final *Peanuts* comic strip was scheduled for February 13, 2000, the day on which he died.

Part G. Commas for Addresses

Practice 13, page 308

The following commas should be added:

1. Their address is 6 Great Ormond Street, London, England.
2. Seattle, Washington, faces the Cascade Mountains.
3. That package must be sent to 30 West Overland Street, Phoenix, Arizona.
4. C
5. His father now lives in Waco, Texas, but his sister has never left Vermont.
6. How far is Kansas City, Kansas, from Independence, Missouri?
7. The old watch factory at 43 North Oak Street, Scranton, Pennsylvania, has been condemned by the building inspector.
8. Foster's Stationery, 483 Heebers Street, Plainview, sells special calligraphy pens.

Part H. Commas for Coordination and Subordination

Practice 15, page 309

The following commas should be added:

1. parts,
2. C
3. crushed,
4. C
5. recycled,
6. time,
7. C
8. easily,
9. parts,
10. benefit,

Chapter Review, page 311

The following comma errors should be corrected:

Treetop Crusader

(1) On December 18, ~~1999~~ *1999,* Julia Butterfly Hill's feet touched ground for the first time in more than two years. (2) She had just climbed down from the ~~top, of~~ *top of* an ancient ~~tree, in~~ *tree in* Humboldt ~~County~~ *County,* California. (3) The ~~tree~~ *tree,* a thousand-year-old ~~redwood~~ *redwood,* was named Luna. (4) Hill had climbed 180 feet up Luna on December ~~10 1997~~ *10, 1997,* for what she thought would be a protest of two or three weeks. (5) Hill's action was intended to stop Pacific ~~Lumber~~ *Lumber,* a division of the Maxxam ~~Corporation~~ *Corporation,* from cutting down old-growth forests. (6) The area immediately next to ~~Luna, had~~ *Luna had* already been stripped of trees. (7) Because nothing was left to hold the soil to the ~~mountain~~ *mountain,* a huge part of the hill had slid into the town of ~~Stafford~~ *Stafford,* California. (8) Many homes had been destroyed.

(9) During her long tree-sit, Hill endured incredible hardships. (10) For more than two ~~years~~ *years,* she ~~lived, on~~ *lived on* a tiny platform eighteen stories off the ground. (11) El Niño storms almost destroyed her with ferocious ~~winds~~ *winds,* razor-sharp ~~rain~~ *rain,* and numbing cold. (12) She once wore two pairs of ~~socks~~ *socks,* ~~booties~~ *booties,* two pairs of thermal ski ~~pants~~ *pants,* two thermal ~~shirts~~ *shirts,* a wool ~~sweater~~ *sweater,* two ~~windbreakers~~ *windbreakers,* a ~~raincoat~~ *raincoat,* ~~gloves~~ *gloves,* and two hats to keep from freezing to death during a storm. (13) In addition to enduring nature's ~~hardships~~ *hardships,* Hill withstood life-threatening torment from the logging company. (14) She was harassed by ~~helicopters~~ *helicopters,* various ~~sieges~~ *sieges,* and interference with receiving supplies. (15) Of ~~course~~ *course,* she also endured ~~loneliness~~ *loneliness,* sometimes paralyzing ~~fear~~ *fear,* and always deep sorrow for the destruction around her.

(16) Only twenty-three at the beginning of her ~~tree-sit~~ *tree-sit,* Hill eventually became both world famous and very knowledgeable about ancient forests. (17) At the top of ~~Luna~~ *Luna,* she would use a cell ~~phone~~ *phone,* a ~~pager~~ *pager,* and a daily engagement planner. (18) She was trying to protect the tree ~~itself~~ *itself,* to slow down all logging in the ~~area~~ *area,* and to raise public awareness. (19) She gave hundreds of phone interviews and answered hundreds of letters.

(20) Hill's action was dramatically successful; Luna was eventually saved from destruction.

(21) When Hill returned to normal *life*, ~~life~~ she wrote a ~~book~~ *book,* *The Legacy of Luna: The Story of a Tree, a Woman, and the Struggle to Save the Redwoods.* (22) Julia Butterfly Hill is now a ~~writer~~ *writer,* a ~~poet~~ *poet,* and an activist. (23) She is a frequent speaker at environmental ~~conferences~~ *conferences,* she helped found the Circle of Life Foundation for preserving all ~~life~~ *life,* and she has received many honors and awards.

Chapter 28 Apostrophes

Part A. Using the Apostrophe for Contractions

Practice 1, page 313

1. you're
2. who's
3. wasn't
4. they're

5. can't
6. it's
7. I'm
8. won't

Practice 2, page 314

The following apostrophes should be added:

1. Won't
2. What's
3. I've
4. You're
5. Who's
6. Aren't

7. we're
8. can't
9. It's
10. Let's
11. Didn't
12. doesn't; don't

Part B. Defining the Possessive

Practice 4, page 314

1. Judson owns the camera
2. the people have hopes
3. the woman owns the thought

4. the home team owns trophies
5. that man has ideas

Part C. Using the Apostrophe to Show Possession (in Words That Do Not Already End in -S)

Practice 5, page 315

1. Rona's eyes
2. the coach's voice
3. Noah's ark

4. tomorrow's technology
5. someone's jacket

Practice 6, page 315

1. Judy's
2. diver's
3. Murphy's
4. Bill's
5. somebody's

6. everyone's
7. daughter's
8. month's
9. woman's
10. anyone's

Part D. Using the Apostrophe to Show Possession (in Words That Already End in -S)

Practice 8, page 316

1. my grandparents' farm
2. my neighbors' kindness
3. the basketball players' dunk shots

4. The Smashing Pumpkins' music
5. the horses' trainer

Practice 9, page 316

1. models'
2. model's
3. pilot's
4. children's
5. runner's
6. Boris'/Boris's

7. niece's
8. parents'
9. men's
10. students'
11. contestants'
12. Jones'/Jones's

Practice 10, page 316

1. Rusty's motorcycle needs new brakes.
2. Nurse Johnson's evidence proved that the doctor was not careless.
3. Ahmad's salary barely keeps him in peanut butter.
4. Lee's job in the Complaint Department keeps him on his toes.
5. José's bad cold makes it hard for him to sleep.
6. Jessie's joke did not make us laugh.
7. John Adams' son was the first president's son to become president of the United States.
8. My sisters' daycare center is open seven days a week.
9. The twins' goal is to learn synchronized swimming.
10. Darren's thank-you note says it all.

Chapter Review, page 318

The following errors should be corrected:

The Magic Fastener

(1) ~~Its~~ *It's* hard to remember the world without Velcro. (2) Shoelaces had to be tied; ~~jackets'~~ *jackets* had to be zipped and ~~did'nt~~ *didn't* make so much noise when they were loosened. (3) We have a Swiss ~~engineers'~~ *engineer's* curiosity to thank for ~~todays~~ *today's* changes.

(4) On a hunting trip in 1948, Georges de Mestral became intrigued by the seedpods that clung

were

to his clothing. (5) He knew that they ~~we're~~ hitching rides to new territory by fastening onto him,

couldn't

but he ~~could'nt~~ tell how they were doing it. (6) He examined the seedpods to find that their tiny

hooks were catching onto the threads of his jacket.

wasn't

(7) The idea of Velcro was born, but the actual product ~~wasnt~~ developed overnight. (8) It took

years   *Mestral's*

eight more ~~years'~~ before Georges de ~~Mestrals~~ invention was ready for the market. (9) Today,

Velcro is used on clothing, on space suits, and even in artificial hearts. (10) Velcro can not only

person's

help keep a skier warm, but it can also save a ~~persons'~~ life.

Chapter 29 Direct and Indirect Quotations

Part A. Defining Direct and Indirect Quotations

Practice 1, page 319

1. I
2. D
3. I

4. D
5. D
6. I

Part B. Punctuating Simple Direct Quotations

Practice 2, page 320

1. He yelled, "Answer the phone!"
2. The usher called, "No more seats in front."
3. "My back aches," she repeated dejectedly.
4. Examining the inside cover, Bob said, "This book was printed in 1879."
5. "A bug is doing the backstroke in my soup," the man said.

Part C. Punctuating Split Quotations

Practice 3, page 321

1. "Before the guests arrive," she said, "let's relax."
2. "Don't drive so fast," he begged. "I get nervous."
3. "Although Mort is out shellfishing," Fran said, "his hip boots are on the porch."
4. "Being the youngest in the family," she said, "has its advantages."
5. "This catalog is fantastic," the clerk said, "and you can have it for free."

Part D. Ending Direct Quotations

Practice 5, page 322

1. Barbara asked, "Is that your Humvee?"
2. "Did Shenoya make the team?" he inquired.
3. "Be careful with that mirror!" she begged the movers.
4. The truck driver shouted, "Give me a break!"
5. Did she say, "I wouldn't give my social security number to that telemarketer"?

Chapter Review, page 323

The following corrections should be made:

Satchel Paige

(1) Some people say that the great pitcher Leroy Paige was called Satchel because of his big feet. (2) Paige himself ~~said I~~ *said, "I* got the nickname as a boy in Mobile before my feet ~~grew.~~ *grew."* (3) He earned money by carrying bags, called satchels, at the railroad station. (4) ~~I~~ *"I* figured out a way to make more money by carrying several bags at a time on a ~~pole~~ *pole,"* he said. (5) Other boys began shouting at him that he looked like a satchel tree. (6) The name stuck.

(7) Unfortunately, for most of Paige's long pitching career, major league baseball excluded African-American players. (8) However, Satchel Paige pitched impressively in the black leagues and in tours against white teams. (9) In 1934, he won a thirteen-inning, one-to-nothing pitching duel against the white pitcher Dizzy Dean and a team of major league all-stars. (10) ~~My~~ *"My* fast ~~ball~~ *ball,"* admitted ~~Dean looks~~ *Dean, "looks* like a change of pace alongside of that little bullet old Satchel shoots up to the ~~plate!~~ *plate!"*

(11) After Jackie Robinson broke the major league color barrier in 1948, Satchel Paige took his windmill windup to the Cleveland Indians. (12) He became the oldest rookie in major league history. (13) Some people said that he was too old, but his record proved them wrong. (14) His plaque in the Baseball Hall of Fame ~~reads he~~ *reads, "He* helped pitch the Cleveland Indians to the 1948 ~~pennant.~~ *pennant."*

(15) Satchel Paige pitched off and on until he was sixty years old. (16) When people asked how he stayed young, he gave them his famous rules. (17) Everyone remembers the last one. (18) ~~Don't~~ *"Don't* look ~~back~~ *back,"* he said. (19) ~~Something~~ *"Something* might be gaining on ~~you.~~ *you."*

Chapter 30 Putting Your Proofreading Skills to Work

Proofreading Practice 1, page 325

The following errors should be corrected:

                                                                                       on   *sprees*
(1) Bono is an unusual superstar. (2) Instead of going ~~in~~ shopping ~~spree~~ and polishing his ego,

                                                                                                                   in
he travels the world, using his fame to empower others. (3) Bono was born Paul Hewson ~~at~~ Ireland.

(4) Young friends there nicknamed him *Bonovox*, which means "good voice" in Latin. (5) The *vox*
        dropped, but bono
was ~~dropped, bono~~ stuck. (6) Bono became the lead singer of the Irish rock band U2. (7) Using music
                                                           sold   *albums*
to send a message of love and peace, U2 has ~~sell~~ more than 100 million ~~album~~ worldwide and has

won fourteen Grammy Awards. (8) Yet perhaps Bono's greatest influence is not the sound of his
                                 inside   *in*
voice crooning U2 songs ~~under~~ the heads of fans. (9) Rather, it is his work for human beings ~~on~~ need.
                          used
(10) Bono has ~~use~~ his celebrity to turn the media's attention to Africa, where the lives of millions
              destroyed   *children*
are being ~~destroy~~ by AIDS and starvation. (11) Frightening numbers of African ~~child~~ are already
              orphans; social
AIDS ~~orphans, social~~ structures in Africa are breaking down. (12) Bono urges the United States and
                                                                                                                        factors
other nations to relieve the crippling debt of African nations, one of the ~~factor~~ that keeps them
                                                                                              worked
unable to afford AIDS drugs and prevention programs. (13) He has ~~work~~ with former President

Clinton, Oprah, and others to make the love he sings about become reality. (14) Bono has received
             awards   *work; he*   *nominated*
many ~~award~~ for this humanitarian ~~work he~~ was even ~~nominate~~ for the Nobel Peace Prize.

Proofreading Practice 2, page 326

The following errors should be corrected:

                                         common that
(1) Flying is so ~~common.~~ (2) ~~That~~ many people take it for granted. (3) They often see jets,

helicopters, and airplanes in the sky and give them little thought. (4) However, what would
                      think if   *saw*   *July*
people ~~think.~~ (5) ~~If~~ they ~~seen~~ a human being flying through the air? (6) In ~~july,~~ 2003, Felix
Baumgartner flew   *English*
~~baumgartner flied~~ across the ~~english~~ Channel without using an engine, something that had never
                                                                 began   *England when*
been done before. (7) His amazing flight ~~begun~~ high above ~~England.~~ (8) ~~When~~ he jumped from an
                      was
airplane at 30,000 feet. (9) He ~~is~~ wearing a parachute, of course, but his other piece of special

equipment was a six-foot-wide wing strapped to his back. (10) Even though he was falling very

needed

quickly, the wing let him fly forward at 220 miles per hour. (11) He ~~needs~~ to fly twenty-two miles

to get to France, and he arrived over that country with 4,000 feet remaining. (12) After using the

down, he   *lasted*

wing to slow himself ~~down.~~ (13) ~~He~~ opened his parachute and landed. (14) The entire flight ~~lasts~~

Skyray,

just six minutes. (15) People who want to experience this kind of flying can use the ~~Skyray.~~

which   *Channel.*

(16) ~~Which~~ is similar to the special wing Baumgartner used to fly across the English ~~channel.~~

(17) Of course, to use this wing, you have to wear a parachute and jump out of an airplane.

(18) Nevertheless, Skyray is bringing humans closer to the dream of flying like eagles.

Proofreading Practice 3, page 327

The following errors should be corrected:

(1) Christiane Amanpour is one of the most respected foreign correspondents in the world, but

journalist" because

she calls herself an "accidental ~~journalist."~~ (2) ~~Because~~ she never intended to become one. (3) Her

press, so journalism

native Iran had no freedom of the ~~press, journalism~~ did not interest her. (4) Christiane attended

father's

high school in England. (5) Then the revolution in Iran brought chaos to her family, her ~~fathers~~

frozen, and   *family's funds*   *Christiane's*

money was ~~froze,~~ the ~~families fund~~ were very tight. (6) ~~Christianes'~~ sister dropped out of

London, and Christiane

journalism college in ~~London, Christiane~~ took her place for the sole reason of saving the tuition

hooked

money. (7) Soon she was ~~hook~~ on reporting. (8) After graduating from the University of Rhode

station called

Island, she applied for a job at a new cable ~~station.~~ (9) ~~Called~~ CNN. (10) She longed to write news

stories   *mocked*

~~story's~~ and go overseas but was ~~mock~~ by her boss, who said she didn't have the right looks and

that her name was difficult to pronounce. (11) Amanpour worked hard and hid her frustration

tasks like

with doing routine ~~task.~~ (12) ~~Like~~ bringing people coffee. (13) Every time a new job opened at

sent

CNN, she applied for it. (14) Her big break was being ~~send~~ to Germany and the Gulf War.

gunfire

(15) With ~~gunfires~~ and rockets around her, she reported the news with intelligence and heart.

(16) Today Amanpour says it is not so bad that some people "always try to knock your dreams."

(17) This gives you the chance, she believes, to prove that you are strong enough to keep going.

Proofreading Practice 4, page 327

The following errors should be corrected:

(1) Every spring and summer, storm *chasers spread* ~~chaser's spreads~~ out across the Midwestern part of the United States known as Tornado Alley. (2) Armed with video *cameras, maps,* ~~cameras maps~~ and *radios, these* ~~radios. (3) These~~ lovers of violent weather *follow* ~~follows~~ huge weather systems called supercells, which sometimes *produce* ~~produces~~ tornadoes. (4) On a good day, a storm chaser may find a *supercell and* ~~supercell. (5) And~~ get close enough to film the brief, destructive life of a tornado. (6) Some *join* ~~joins~~ the storm-chasing tours offered every summer by universities or private companies. (7) Others learn what they can from Internet websites and *set* ~~sets~~ off on their own to hunt tornadoes. (8) Storm chasing can be very dangerous. (9) A large tornado spins winds between 125 and 175 mph, tearing roofs off *houses,* ~~houses~~ ripping limbs from trees, and overturning cars. (10) The greatest danger comes from airborne *branches, boards, shingles,* ~~branches boards shingles~~ and glass hurtling through the air like deadly weapons. (11) Even if a supercell *doesn't* ~~don't~~ spawn *tornadoes, it* ~~tornadoes. (12) It~~ often produces winds over 50 mph, heavy rain, large hail, and intense lightning. (13) Most storm chasers *avoid* ~~avoids~~ these risks by racing out of a *tornado's* ~~tornados'~~ path before it gets too close. (14) Despite or perhaps because of these dangers, dramatized in the 1996 movie *Twister, storm* ~~Twister. (15) Storm~~ chasing remains popular. (16) Fans claim that few things in life *match* ~~matches~~ the thrill of discovering a tornado and witnessing the power of nature.

Proofreading Practice 5, page 329

The following errors should be corrected:

(1) A secret society called SSSSH is gaining agents across the country. (2) To become a secret agent, one must simply perform a *good* ~~well~~ deed for someone without taking credit for it or letting *him or her* ~~them~~ know who did it. (3) The group was inspired by a young Ohioan named *Hal Reichle* ~~hal reichle~~ (pronounced "Rike-el"), a graduate of *Hiram College,* ~~hiram college~~ who had a habit of *quietly* ~~quiet~~ helping people. (4) After Hal's death in a helicopter crash during the *Gulf War,* ~~gulf War~~ some friends started paying tribute to the fallen soldier by "pulling Reichles." (5) That is, they would do small or large good deeds, leaving only a

anonymous
card that said, "You are the recipient of an ~~anonymously~~ good deed done in the name of Hal

itself
Reichle." (6) The group called ~~themselves~~ SSSSH, or Secret Society of Serendipitous Service to

Hal. (7) After several newspapers wrote about the secret society, school children and people in

themselves   *he or she*
other states began to pull Reichles ~~theirselves~~. (8) If an agent wants to report, ~~they~~ can write

about the deed performed—without a signature or return address, of course—to Hal Reichle, P.O.
375, Hiram, Ohio   *who*
Box ~~375 Hiram ohio~~ 44234. (9) A friend of Hal's ~~whom~~ claimed to know only that SSSSH exists but

nothing more said that the goal of the organization is a simple one: increasing goodness in the

world.

Proofreading Practice 6, page 329

The following errors should be corrected:

Crime-Fighting Artist

America's   *criminals,*
(1) Jeanne Boylan helps capture ~~Americas~~ most wanted ~~criminals~~ but she's not a police officer
based
or a detective. (2) Instead, she is an artist who draws the faces of suspects, ~~base~~ only on her gentle
victims
conversations with ~~victim's~~ and eyewitnesses. (3) Her portraits are so lifelike and accurate that
become
she has ~~became~~ famous for drawing nearly mirror images of criminals. (4) Boylan's sketches often
lead
~~leads~~ to arrests. (5) She drew the Unabomber in his sunglasses and hooded sweatshirt, the
McVeigh, who
kidnapper-murderer of twelve-year-old Polly Klaas, and Timothy ~~McVeigh.~~ (6) ~~Who~~ bombed
call
Oklahoma City's Federal Building. (7) Once doubtful, FBI officials and police now ~~calls on~~

Boylan in almost every major case.

(8) Boylan decided to become a sketch artist after she was the victim of a crime. (9) The
faces; then
police, following standard procedure, asked her to describe her attackers' ~~faces, then~~ they showed
criminals, hoping
her mug shots of ~~criminals.~~ (10) ~~Hoping~~ that she would recognize the suspects. (11) Boylan sensed

that this was the wrong approach to help her mind remember. (12) She realized that the
authorities'
~~authorities~~ leading questions—questions like "Did he have a moustache? Was he wearing

glasses?"—clutter the victim's mind with details that might not be true. (13) At the same time, *experience;*

the subconscious mind is trying to avoid reliving a traumatic ~~experience~~ consequently, memories

easily become distorted.

(14) Boylan developed a very different method for coaxing images from victims and

witnesses. (15) What distinguishes her method from others, she says, is that she *listens.* (16) She

time, talking

takes her ~~time.~~ (17) ~~Talking~~ for hours with eyewitnesses to a crime. (18) She does not pressure

them to recall the color of a suspect's eyes or ~~what~~ the shape of his nose ~~was.~~ (19) Instead, she

asks about their daily lives and interests, here and there asking non-leading questions about what

carefully,

they saw. (20) Slowly and ~~careful,~~ she guides people back through their confusion and pain to the

saw

moment when they ~~seen~~ or felt something that they desperately want to forget. (21) She asks

them to describe whole shapes, forms, and textures rather than specific details. (22) She

sometimes gives children Play-Doh to mold as they explore their memories. (23) As they draw

minds,

closer and closer to the terrifying images seared into their ~~minds.~~ (24) Boylan watches, listens,

sketches.

and ~~sketching.~~ (25) "What people see," she says, "is evidence as fragile and valuable as a

fingerprint. (26) And it should be protected with as much care."

(27) Many have claimed that Boylan's method, a blend of art, psychology, and human

is   *taught.*

compassion, ~~are~~ a unique gift. (28) Boylan insists, though, that her technique can be ~~teach.~~

mystery,"

(29) "What I do is no great ~~mystery~~ she says. (30) "It has to do with allowing someone the freedom

and the time to remember. (31) It has to do with the human heart."

Proofreading Practice 7, page 331

The following errors should be corrected:

Quiet, Please!

pierce   *air; car*

(1) America is loud. (2) Horns and sirens ~~pierces~~ the ~~air, car~~ stereos pump out loud music.

ring   *trumpet*   *equipment*

(3) Cell phones ~~rings,~~ shriek, or ~~trumpets~~ the owner's noise of choice. (4) Construction ~~equipments,~~

lawnmowers, and leaf blowers buzz and roar into the public space. (5) Restaurant and movie

managers

theater ~~manager's~~ often seem to link loudness with cultural cool. (6) Sounds are measured in

decibels;
decibels, with the human voice measuring about 60 ~~decibels~~, the sound of a car is about 80 decibels.

(7) According to the U.S. Environmental Protection Agency, 70 decibels is a safe daily average.

is
(8) Here is the problem: the level of noise that many of us hear every day ~~are~~ far above this.

blowers
(9) The sound of a food blender, for example, measures 90 decibels. (10) Many leaf ~~blower~~

exceed 115 decibels, and a jet taking off is 120 decibels of ear-blasting noise. (11) All of this racket
is   *its*   *psychologically*
~~are~~ taking ~~it's~~ toll on us both physically and ~~in psychological ways~~. (12) According to the

American Speech-Language-Hearing Association (ASHA), 28 million U.S. citizens have already
suffered   *pressure,*
~~suffer~~ hearing loss from too much noise. (13) Furthermore, loud noise raises blood ~~pressure~~ increases

stress hormone levels, and deprives us of sleep. (14) Noise pollution also increases aggression and
York
even violence and hinders concentration and learning. (15) One study found that New ~~york~~

children in classrooms that faced the train tracks were almost a year behind children taught in
quieter
~~more quieter~~ parts of the same school.
seriously
(16) In Europe, noise pollution has been taken ~~serious~~ for years. (17) Now in the United
are
States, organizations like the Noise Pollution Clearinghouse ~~is~~ trying to raise awareness of the
believe
problem and promote solutions. (18) Members of this organization ~~believes~~ that just as smoke or
laws
toxins in the air are not acceptable, neither is loud noise. (19) They are working for new ~~laws~~.
to
(20) ~~To~~ enforce our right to peace and quiet.

Unit 7 Review

Proofreading A, page 334

The following corrections should be made:

Somers Street
99 ~~somers street~~
            Ohio
Northfield, ~~ohio~~ 44056
January
~~january~~ 11, 2005

Weird Walt's
~~weird walts~~ Discount Store
   Office
Main ~~office~~
Akron
~~akron~~, Ohio 44313
  Sir
Dear ~~sir~~ or Madam:
    January 5, 2005,
   On ~~january 5 2005~~ I ordered a Panasonic forty-two-inch plasma flat panel television with a
                        Avenue, Medina, Ohio
remote control from your store at 1101 Lakeland ~~avenue medina ohio~~. The model number is

TH42PX20UP. When your delivery man brought the set to my home yesterday, he seemed
                        box, unpack it,
impatient. He urged me to sign before I had a chance to open the ~~box unpack it~~ or examine the
              buddy, I've   *I'm*
equipment. In fact, he said, "Listen, ~~buddy Ive~~ got five more deliveries, and ~~Im~~ out of here
        not."   *dismay,*
whether you open the box or ~~not~~. To my ~~dismay~~ I later discovered that the hand-held remote

control was missing.
                        Panasonic
   Please send me this remote control immediately. I purchased this ~~panasonic~~ in time to use it
  Bowl   *now,*
at my Super ~~bowl~~ party. Obviously, my friends and I will need the remote control. For years ~~now~~ I
          Walt's
have been a loyal customer at Weird ~~Walts~~ and will appreciate your prompt attention to this
  Thank
matter. ~~thank~~ you.

                       yours
                  Sincerely ~~your's~~,
                  Rainford
                  Milton ~~rainford~~

Proofreading B, page 335

The following corrections should be made:

The Liberator of South America

(1) One day in ~~1805~~ *1805,* Simón Bolívar made a vow. (2) He vowed that he ~~wouldnt~~ *wouldn't* rest until South America was free from ~~spanish~~ *Spanish* oppression. (3) This promise changed his life and Latin American ~~history~~ *history.* (4) ~~Bolívar~~ *Bolívar,* surprisingly ~~enough~~ *enough,* spent the first twenty-two years of his life as a rich aristocrat. (5) When he died at ~~fifty-seven~~ *fifty-seven,* he was known as the ~~george~~ *George* Washington of ~~south america~~ *South America.*

(6) Bolívar was born in ~~caracas, Venezuela~~ *Caracas, Venezuela,* on July ~~24~~ *24,* 1783. (7) ~~after~~ *After* he became an orphan at the age of ~~nine~~ *nine,* his uncle provided him with a ~~tutor~~ *tutor,* Simón ~~Rodriguez~~ *Rodriguez.* (8) A fierce ~~patriot~~ *patriot,* Rodriguez wanted South ~~American's~~ *Americans* to rule themselves. (9) ~~However~~ *However,* young Simón Bolívar ~~was'nt~~ *wasn't* very interested in his ~~tutors~~ *tutor's* ideas about independence. (10) ~~Bolívars~~ *Bolívar's* uncle sent Simón to ~~europe~~ *Europe* to help further the young ~~mans~~ *man's* education. (11) ~~during~~ *During* his travels in Spain, Bolívar realized that Latin America was destined to be independent of Spain.

(12) Bolívar returned to Venezuela and joined those fighting Spain. (13) His troops were ~~defeated~~ *defeated,* but Bolívar would not admit to failure. (14) In a famous letter that he wrote in 1814, he declared, ~~"the~~ *"The* bonds that unite us to Spain have been ~~cut".~~ *cut."* (15) Finally, the tide turned against Spain. (16) The ~~spaniards~~ *Spaniards* were driven out of ~~Colombia Venezuela Ecuador~~ *Colombia, Venezuela, Ecuador,* Peru, and ~~Bolivia~~ *Bolivia.* (17) Bolívar, leader of much of South ~~America~~ *America,* wanted to unite the people under one government. (18) His idea may have been a good ~~one~~ *one,* yet each area preferred to become a separate nation. (19) Although his plan for a united country ~~failed~~ *failed,* Bolívar is still remembered as South ~~Americas~~ *America's* greatest hero.

Unit 7 Writers' Workshop, page 336

1. Y   Y
   Y   Y
2. Paragraph 1, sentence 4
6. time order
7. Five comma splices

UNIT 8
Improving Your Spelling

Chapter 31 Spelling

Part B. Computer Spell Checkers

Practice 1, page 341

I   have   checker,
~~Eye halve~~ a spelling ~~check her~~,

                    PC.
It came with my ~~pea see~~.

            marks   for   review,
It clearly ~~marques four~~ my ~~revue~~,

Mistakes   I   cannot   see.
~~Miss steaks eye kin knot sea~~.

                through
I've run this poem ~~threw~~ it.

        sure you're pleased to know.
I'm ~~shore your please too no~~.

It's   its   way.
~~Its~~ letter perfect in ~~it's weigh~~.

            told   so.
My checker ~~tolled~~ me ~~sew~~.

Part C. Spotting Vowels and Consonants

Practice 2, page 342

1. C C V C V
2. C V C C
3. C V C V
4. C V C C
5. C V C C V C
6. C V C C V C

Part D. Doubling the Final Consonant (in Words of One Syllable)

Practice 3, page 342

Last Three Letters	-ed	-ing
1. cvc	planned	planning
2. cvc	bragged	bragging
3. cvc	dipped	dipping
4. vvc	sailed	sailing
5. cvc	stopped	stopping

Practice 4, page 343

Last Three Letters	-er	-est
1. vcc	taller	tallest
2. vcc	shorter	shortest
3. cvc	fatter	fattest
4. cvc	slimmer	slimmest
5. cvc	wetter	wettest
6. vcc	quicker	quickest

Part E. Doubling the Final Consonant (in Words of More Than One Syllable)

Practice 5, page 344

Last Three Letters	-ed	-ing
1. cvc	occurred	occurring
2. cvc	happened	happening
3. vcc	polished	polishing
4. cvc	committed	committing
5. cvc	offered	offering
6. cvc	preferred	preferring
7. cvc	exited	exiting
8. cvc	traveled	traveling
9. cvc	wondered	wondering
10. cvc	omitted	omitting

Practice 6, page 344

1. worked
2. enrolled
4. depended
5. compelled, performing
6. obtained
7. hoped
8. admitted, getting
9. retiring
10. asked
11. permitted
12. demanded, starring
13. planned
14. stopped, preferred
15. winning, astonishing
16. proclaimed

Part F. Dropping or Keeping the Final E

Practice 7, page 346

1. blameless
2. guidance
3. debating
4. motivation
5. sincerely
6. desirable
7. argument
8. homeless
9. responsible
10. rejoicing
11. awful
12. manager
13. judgment
14. famous
15. grievance
16. arranging

Part G. Changing or Keeping the Final Y

Practice 8, page 347

1. cried
2. merciful
3. worrying
4. said
5. juicier
6. enjoyable
7. clumsiness
8. wealthiest
9. daily
10. merrily

Practice 9, page 347

1. livelier, liveliest, liveliness
2. beautify, beautiful, beauties
3. healthier, healthiest, healthily
4. studies, studious, studying
5. business, busier, busiest
6. tries, tried, trial

Practice 10, page 347

1. tried, hungrier, sleepier, angrier, lonelier
2. denial, business, pleasurable
3. fascinating
4. immediately, similarities, displayed
5. primarily, exposure, mercilessly
6. Happily
7. fatigued
8. exercising, changing, noticeable
9. guidance
10. healthiest

Part H. Choosing IE *or* EI

Practice 11, page 348

1. field
2. weight
3. neither
4. weird
5. chief
6. seize
7. receive
8. brief

9. height
10. achieve
11. efficient
12. vein
13. their
14. foreign
15. cashier

Chapter Review, page 350

The following spelling corrections should be made:

A Precious Resource

(1) Many people have pleasant ~~memorys~~ *memories* of ~~recieving~~ *receiving* their first library card or ~~chooseing~~ *choosing* books for the first time at a local public library. (2) Widely recognized as a priceless resource, the public library is defined just as you might expect: a collection of books and other materials supported by the public for public use.

(3) Several New England towns claim the honor of ~~contributeing~~ *contributing* the first public money for a library. (4) However, the first such library of meaningful size and influence—the first ~~fameous~~ *famous* public library—originated in Boston, Massachusetts, in 1854. (5) The Boston Public Library, with its useful ~~refrence~~ *reference* collection and its policy of ~~circulateing~~ *circulating* popular books, set the pattern for all public ~~librarys~~ *libraries* ultimately created in the United States and Canada. (6) By the end of the nineteenth century, many state ~~goverments~~ *governments* were ~~begining~~ *beginning* to raise taxes to support libraries. (7) They ~~beleived~~ *believed* that public libraries had an extremely ~~importent~~ *important* role in helping people pursue ~~knowlege~~ *knowledge* and continue ~~thier~~ *their* education. (8) Although public ~~libaries~~ *libraries* today have much the same goal, they now offer a ~~truely admireable~~ *truly admirable* number of resources and services. (9) These include story hours for children, book discussion clubs for adults, ~~intresting~~ *interesting* lectures, art exhibits, literacy classes, and most recently, computer training and ~~guideance~~ *guidance*.

(10) Technology, of course, has transformed the management of the public library, as well as

the way the library is used. (11) The ~~bigest~~ *biggest* changes—today's computerized catalogs, searchable

databases, and Internet access—would ~~definately~~ *definitely* have gone beyond the wildest dreams of even

the most ~~commited~~ *committed* early public ~~libary~~ *library* supporters.

Chapter 32 Look-Alikes/Sound-Alikes

Practice 1, page 353

1. a
2. a, an
3. and, a
4. and, a

5. A, and
6. a
7. a, and
8. an, and, a

Practice 2, page 354

1. accept
2. accept
3. except
4. accepted

5. except
6. Except
7. except
8. except, accept

Practice 3, page 354

1. been
2. being
3. been
4. been

5. being
6. been
7. being
8. being, been

Practice 4, page 355

1. buy
2. by
3. by, buy
4. by

5. buy
6. by
7. buy
8. by

Practice 5, page 355

1. fine
2. find
3. find

4. fine
5. fine
6. find

Practice 6, page 356

1. it's
2. It's
3. its
4. It's
5. It's

6. its
7. It's
8. it's
9. It's
10. it's, its

Practice 7, page 356

1. new
2. know
3. know, new
4. knew
5. know, new

6. no, know
7. knew
8. no
9. know
10. knew, know

Practice 8, page 357

1. loose
2. lose
3. loose, lose
4. loose

5. loose
6. lose
7. lose
8. lose, loose

Practice 9, page 357

1. mine
2. mind
3. mind
4. mind

5. mind
6. mind
7. mind
8. mine, mind

Practice 10, page 358

1. passed
2. past
3. passed
4. passed

5. passed
6. past
7. past
8. passed, past

Practice 11, page 358

1. quite
2. quiet
3. quite
4. quiet
5. quits

6. quiet
7. quit
8. quite
9. quiet, quite
10. quit

Practice 12, page 359

1. rises
2. raised
3. rose
4. rise
5. raise

6. rise
7. raised
8. raised
9. risen
10. rose

Practice 13, page 360

1. set
2. sit
3. Set
4. sits/sat

5. set
6. Sit, set
7. set
8. sat, sit

Practice 14, page 360

1. suppose
2. supposed
3. suppose
4. suppose
5. supposed

6. supposed
7. suppose
8. supposed
9. supposed
10. suppose

Practice 15, page 361

1. there
2. There
3. they're
4. their, there
5. They're

6. there
7. They're, their
8. Their
9. there
10. they're, they're

Practice 16, page 362

1. than
2. than
3. then
4. than

5. then
6. then
7. than
8. then

Practice 17, page 362

1. through
2. threw
3. threw

4. through
5. through
6. through

Practice 18, page 363

1. to, two
2. too, to
3. to, too
4. too, to, to
5. too

6. to, two, to
7. to, to
8. too
9. too, to
10. two, to

Practice 19, page 363

1. used
2. used
3. use
4. used
5. use

6. used
7. use
8. used
9. use, used
10. used

Practice 20, page 364

1. weather
2. whether
3. whether
4. weather

5. whether
6. whether
7. whether
8. whether, weather

Practice 21, page 364

1. we're
2. Where
3. were
4. were, where
5. where

6. were, where
7. Were, we're
8. were, where, were
9. where
10. Where, we're, we're

Practice 22, page 365

1. Who's
2. Whose
3. whose
4. Who's

5. whose
6. whose
7. who's, who's
8. Who's

Practice 23, page 365

1. your
2. you're
3. your
4. your
5. you're, your

6. Your
7. your
8. You're, your
9. you're
10. your, you're

Chapter Review, page 367

The following corrections should be made:

Rapper with a Difference

(1) If ~~you're~~ *your* concept of hip-hop music is gang fights, drugs, the fast life, and negative views of women, ~~than~~ *then* perhaps you haven't heard of Wyclef Jean. (2) Like many rappers, Jean is committed to making music with powerful lyrics and driving rhythms. (3) However, this Haitian-born former Fugee sends a very different message and lives a ~~quiter~~ *quieter* lifestyle than many hip-hop artists do.

(4) Unlike some hip-hop music—named "gangsta rap" for ~~it's~~ *its* glorification of violence—Jean's songs celebrate nonviolence and understanding. (5) For example, in his fourth solo album, *The Preacher's Son*, Jean shares his vision of a peaceful world ~~were~~ *where* everyone gets along. (6) He believes that if people can ~~set~~ *sit* and talk, they can work ~~though~~ *through* almost anything. (7) Wyclef pleads for an end to dangerous feuds between rappers, such as the clashes between 50 Cent and Ja

past
Rule, Jay-Z and Nas, and the ~~passed~~ rivalry, kept alive in music, between Tupac Shakur and

their
Notorious B.I.G., both gunned down in ~~there~~ prime.

(8) Jean also differs from other rappers in his calm lifestyle. (9) While many hip-hop

celebrities live the high life, traveling with bodyguards and a posse of companions, the down-to-

earth Jean insists on strolling the streets by himself. (10) He says he does not want to become

by   *it's*
disconnected from reality ~~buy~~ cutting himself off from it. (11) So ~~its~~ not unusual to see Jean standing

on a street corner talking with a homeless person or bonding with a young thug who tried to rob

him moments before.

being
(12) Now Jean is ~~been~~ seen as a role model by a new generation of hip-hop artists and fans.

(13) One of his passions is Clef's Kids, an after-school music program, for music is a vehicle to his

used
higher goal of changing the world. (14) Jean's preacher father, now deceased, ~~use~~ to urge him to

to
study theology, ~~too~~ which Jean replied, "I am just a messenger in a different way."

Unit 8 Review

Proofreading, page 371

The following corrections should be made:

Nature's Weed Whackers

interested
(1) If you raise goats mostly for milk and wool, you might be <u>intrested</u> in this new idea.
liveing   *by*   *cities*
(2) Your goats can earn a <u>liveing</u> just <u>buy</u> eating! (3) Parks, <u>citys</u>, and other businesses are now using
separate   *similar*   *reducing*
goats in three <u>seperate</u> but <u>similer</u> ways. (4) Goats are <u>reduceing</u> forest fires, clearing overgrown
fields   *through*
<u>feilds</u>, and protecting native plants—all <u>threw</u> eating.
than   *branches*
(5) Goats like nothing better <u>then</u> chomping on tons of weeds and <u>branchs</u>. (6) They are

lawnmowers with legs, and, unlike human workers, they don't mind thorns or poisonous plants.
and   *where*
(7) They scale steep hills easily <u>an</u> get into places <u>were</u> mowers can't go. (8) They work without
Finally,
the noise of chain saws. (9) <u>Finaly</u>, goats fertilize the land as they work.

(10) When goats reduce the vegetation in an area, they greatly reduce the intensity of fires.

two inches

(11) If grasses are three feet tall, they create a fifteen-foot-high fire wall that moves at fifteen miles an hour. (12) If grasses are only <u>too inchs</u> tall, they create a one-foot fire wall that moves at three miles an hour.

foreign   *enemies*

(13) Goats have been hired to eat <u>foriegn</u> weeds and plants that have no natural <u>enemys</u>.

countries   *taking*

(14) These plants, which were brought from other <u>countrys</u>, are completely <u>takeing</u> over the

necessity

native plants of some areas. (15) The use of goats avoids the <u>nesessity</u> for using poisonous

cutting   trimming

herbicides or for <u>cuting</u> and <u>triming</u> by hand.

carefully

(16) However, unless goats are managed <u>carfully</u>, they can turn the thickest forest or

important   *your*

countryside into a desert. (17) If you accept this <u>importent</u> new work for <u>youre</u> goats, you must

performing   too

prevent them from <u>purforming</u> their job <u>to</u> well!

Unit 8 Writers' Workshop, page 372

1. Y   Y
    Y/N (see #3 below) N
2. Sentence 2
3. No, change thesis to match body or vice versa; friendliness, playfulness, helpfulness
4. Add a conclusion.
5. No

APPENDIX 2
Some Guidelines for Students of English as a Second Language

Count and Noncount Nouns

Practice 1, page 438

The following plural count nouns should be listed:

1. mountains
4. students
6. men
7. assignments

Practice 2, page 439

The following sentence is correct:

4. We have *an* answer to your question.

Practice 3, page 440

The following sentences are correct:

2. *The* beauty of this building surprises me.
3. This building has *the* beauty of a work of art.

Verb + Gerund/Preposition + Gerund

Practice 4, page 441

The following gerunds are possible answers:

1. watching
2. studying
3. flying
4. celebrating
5. leasing

Practice 5, page 442

The following gerunds are possible answers:

1. finding
2. turning
3. buying
4. canoeing, kayaking
5. going, working, relaxing

Verb + Infinitive

Practice 6, page 442

The following infinitives are possible answers:

1. to fix
2. to take
3. to be
4. to begin
5. to see

Verb + Either Gerund or Infinitive

Practice 7, page 443

The following infinitives and gerunds are possible answers:

1. Infinitive: to wait
   Gerund: waiting

2. Infinitive: to cook
   Gerund: cooking

3. Infinitive: to sing
   Gerund: singing

4. Infinitive: to rumble
   Gerund: rumbling

5. Infinitive: to clap
   Gerund: clapping